MILES J. CORAVEL

Japan Travel Guide

Discover All The Top Attractions, Restaurants, Secret Spots, Fun Facts and 100 Tips for an Unforgettable Adventure

This book was professionally typeset on Reedsy.
Find out more at reedsy.com

Contents

1

Introduction

Welcome, adventurous soul, to your gateway into the land of the rising sun—Japan. Imagine walking the bustling streets of Tokyo, where the future meets tradition, or finding serenity in the Zen gardens of Kyoto, each step unfolding a story centuries old. This isn't just another travel guide; it's your personal compass to discovering Japan's heart and soul, from its neon-lit cities to its tranquil countryside.

Why this book, you ask? Let's face it: traveling can be overwhelming. The internet is a maze of endless information, and too often, we find ourselves lost in a sea of travel blogs, reviews, and itineraries. That's where I come in. I was once a bewildered traveler, just like you, searching for that perfect blend of adventure and authenticity without breaking the bank. After countless trips to Japan, each more enlightening than the last, I've compiled this no-fluff, easy-to-use pocket guide to ensure your journey is nothing short of extraordinary.

This book is your ticket to experiencing Japan beyond the typical tourist traps. You'll feast on the most delectable dishes Japan has to offer, from street food stalls in Osaka to high-end sushi in Tokyo. You'll uncover hidden gems tucked away in bustling cities and quiet towns, places that even Google Maps would struggle to reveal. And let's not forget the people, the soul of Japan, whose stories and kindness will touch your heart in unexpected ways.

Here's a sneak peek of what's inside:

- **Pre-Trip Planning and What to Expect:** Get the lowdown on the essentials, from navigating Japan's transport system to understanding local customs that will save you from those awkward gaijin moments.

- **Getting Settled Once You Arrive:** Tips and tricks to hit the ground running, ensuring your first hours in Japan are as smooth as a bullet train ride.
- **The Foods of Japan:** Your culinary compass to the must-try dishes and where to find them, making each meal an adventure in itself.
- **Best Restaurants in Japan:** From hole-in-the-wall eateries to Michelin-starred experiences, discover where to indulge in Japan's gastronomic delights.
- **Secret Spots:** Unveil the hidden wonders of Japan, places that remain off the tourist radar but are cherished by locals.
- **Top Attractions:** Navigate through Japan's most iconic sights, understanding the stories behind them.
- **Day Trips:** Venture beyond the city limits into the scenic countryside, where tradition and nature harmonize.
- **Fun Facts and Unique Experiences:** Immerse yourself in the quirky, the quaint, and the quintessentially Japanese moments that make for the best stories.
- **100 Tips for an Unforgettable Adventure:** Arm yourself with insider knowledge to elevate your travel experience from great to unforgettable.

Whether you're a solo wanderer, embarking on a romantic getaway, or navigating the adventure with your family, this guide is designed to cater to your curiosity and your budget. Japan is a treasure trove of experiences, and with this book in hand, you're set to unlock them all. As we transition into the heart of this guide, remember that traveling is about more than just visiting new places. It's about the people you meet, the food you taste, and the moments of awe that take your breath away. Japan offers all this and more. So, pack your bags, bring an open heart, and let's embark on this journey together. The next chapter is just the beginning, and I promise, it's going to be an unforgettable adventure.

2

Pre-Trip Planning and What to Expect

E mbarking on a journey to Japan, a land of enchanting contrasts and endless discovery, requires a dash of preparation and a sprinkle of insight. Fear not, for this chapter is your trusty

4

roadmap, guiding you through the essential pre-trip planning steps. From booking your flights to deciding how long to stay, consider this your prelude to an adventure of a lifetime.

Booking Your Flights

The journey to Japan is more than a mere transition from one place to another; it's the exciting onset of your adventure in a land where each vista tells a story. When it comes to booking your flights, strategic planning can enhance your experience right from the start, ensuring you not only arrive with ease but are also greeted by Japan's exquisite landscapes through your window.

Securing the Best Airfare: Preferred Airlines and Timing: Opt for reputable airlines such as ANA (All Nippon Airways), Japan Airlines (JAL), Delta, and Singapore Airlines for a blend of quality service and reasonable pricing on flights to Japan. Mid-week flights—specifically on Tuesdays, Wednesdays, and Thursdays—are typically more affordable and less crowded, potentially saving you around 20-30% compared to weekend travel.

Booking Insights: Whether you're an early planner or a last-minute booker, the golden period to book your flight is about 2-3 months in advance. This window often offers the ideal compromise between competitive pricing and flight selection. Stay vigilant for promotional sales and consider using fare comparison tools that notify you of dips in prices for your desired travel dates.

Airport Arrival and Subsequent Travel: Upon landing, Japan's world-renowned public transit system is ready to whisk you into the heart of its cities:

- **Trains:** From Narita Airport to Tokyo, the JR Narita Express (N'EX) costs around ¥3,000 ($22 USD) for a one-way ticket, offering scenic urban landscapes en route. Haneda Airport's connection via the Tokyo Monorail to the Yamanote Line is about ¥500 ($3.70 USD).
- **Buses:** The Airport Limousine Bus serves as a direct link to key locations in Tokyo and surrounding areas, with fares ranging from ¥1,000 to ¥3,200 ($7.40 to $23.70 USD), blending convenience with the chance to see the city unfold before you.
- **Taxis and Rideshares:** Although offering door-to-door convenience, these options are pricier, with fares easily starting from ¥7,000 ($52 USD) from Haneda to central Tokyo and significantly more from Narita, making them a luxurious but less economical choice.

Cost Efficiency and Practicality: Trains and buses not only provide an economical route into the city (approximately $7 to $24 USD), but they also allow for an immediate immersion into the Japanese landscape. In contrast, taxis, while offering personal space and direct service, are a costlier alternative, suitable for those prioritizing comfort or traveling in groups.

Embracing Japan's Natural Beauty from Above: Choosing a daytime flight can transform your arrival into an aerial tour of Japan's natural splendor. Winter mornings may unveil the snow-capped peak of Mt. Fuji, a serene greeting from Japan's iconic landmark, especially visible on routes from the U.S. West Coast. Spring and autumn flights are a canvas of changing colors, with cherry blossoms and fall foliage creating a mesmerizing patchwork below.

Strategic Seating for Optimal Views: For the best chances of witnessing these landscapes, book a window seat on the plane's right side when flying from North America or Europe. Arriving in the early morning maximizes the likelihood of clear skies, offering unobstructed views of the scenery that make for an unforgettable start to your journey.

Arriving from Outside the US

Traveling to Japan from distant shores requires more than just packing your bags and boarding a plane. It's about preparing for a seamless entry into a country rich with tradition, innovation, and beauty. This section will guide you through the essentials of visas, entry requirements, and additional documentation, ensuring your journey begins without a hitch, regardless of where your journey starts.

Understanding Visa Requirements: Japan's visa policies vary significantly based on your country of origin, dictating the documents you'll need for entry. Most travelers from over 68 countries, including the United States, Canada, Australia, and many European nations, benefit from Japan's visa exemption program, allowing for tourist stays of up to 90 days without a visa. However, if you're planning a longer visit or your country isn't part of this program, you'll need to apply for a visa beforehand.

Specific Requirements for Certain Countries: Travelers from countries not covered by the visa exemption need to prepare additional documents for their visa application. This typically includes a valid passport, a completed visa application form, a recent photograph, and proof of a return ticket or onward journey. In some cases, you might also need to provide evidence of sufficient funds for your stay, and occasionally, a letter of invitation if you're visiting friends or family.

For citizens of China, the Philippines, Vietnam, and Russia, among others, the process can be more stringent, requiring more detailed documentation and potentially an in-person interview at the nearest Japanese embassy or consulate.

Special Regulations and Recommendations

- **Health and Safety Measures:** Given the global health landscape's unpredictability, Japan may implement temporary health screening procedures at entry points or require proof of vaccination against certain diseases. Always check the latest health advisories and entry requirements before your trip.
- **Cultural Considerations:** While not a requirement, understanding basic Japanese customs and phrases can significantly enhance your interaction with immigration officials and your overall entry experience. A simple "Arigato" (thank you) can go a long way.
- **Insurance:** Though not mandatory for entry, travel insurance covering medical expenses is highly recommended. Japan's healthcare is excellent but can be costly for tourists without coverage.

Upon Arrival: Once you land, you'll go through immigration and customs. Keep your passport, visa (if applicable), and any other required documents handy, including your customs declaration form, usually provided during your flight. The process is typically straightforward, but patience is key during peak travel seasons when queues can be longer.

Staying Informed: Regulations can change, so it's crucial to consult the official website of the Japanese embassy or consulate in your country for the most current information before your trip. This ensures you're up-to-date on any new requirements or changes to the visa process, helping you avoid any unnecessary surprises upon arrival.

By familiarizing yourself with these entry requirements and preparing accordingly, you're setting the stage for a smooth start to your Japanese adventure. Whether you're drawn by the promise of bustling cities, serene landscapes, or cultural riches, ensuring your documentation is in order is the first step toward immersing yourself in all that Japan has to offer.

Budgeting for Your Trip

A journey to Japan is a venture into a land of both timeless tradition and cutting-edge modernity. While it offers experiences that can cater to every budget, careful planning and smart budgeting are key to enjoying all that Japan has to offer without financial worry. This section will guide you through estimating your daily expenses, offering tips on how to save money, and providing specific price ranges to help you plan your budget effectively.

Daily Budget Breakdown:

1. **Accommodation:** Costs can vary widely depending on the type of accommodation. Budget travelers can find hostels and guesthouses starting at ¥2,000 to ¥5,000 ($15 to $37 USD) per night. Mid-range hotel prices range from ¥8,000 to ¥20,000 ($59 to $148 USD) per night, while luxury accommodations can start from ¥30,000 ($222 USD) per night upwards.
2. **Food:** Japan's culinary scene offers options for every palate and budget. You can enjoy a filling bowl of ramen or curry rice for about ¥800 to ¥1,200 ($6 to $9 USD). A meal at a mid-range restaurant might cost between ¥2,000 to ¥4,000 ($15 to $30 USD), while fine dining experiences start from ¥10,000 ($74 USD) per

person.

3. **Transportation:** The cost of transportation varies by city and distance. A one-day pass for Tokyo's subway system costs about ¥800 ($6 USD), offering unlimited rides. For intercity travel, consider the Japan Rail Pass, priced at around ¥29,650 ($220 USD) for 7 days, offering unlimited access to JR trains and select buses and ferries.

4. **Sightseeing:** Many temples, shrines, and parks in Japan are free to enter. Museum and garden entry fees range from ¥500 to ¥2,000 ($4 to $15 USD). Special tours and experiences, like tea ceremonies or sumo wrestling matches, can cost anywhere from ¥2,000 to ¥10,000 ($15 to $74 USD) depending on the activity.

5. **Shopping and Souvenirs:** Allocate a portion of your budget for souvenirs and unique Japanese items. Prices vary widely depending on what you buy, but setting aside ¥5,000 to ¥10,000 ($37 to $74 USD) can cover basic souvenirs and gifts.

Money-Saving Tips:

- **Eat Like a Local:** Conveyor belt sushi, department store basements (depachika), and convenience stores offer delicious meals at a fraction of restaurant prices.
- **Stay in Business Hotels or Capsule Hotels:** These offer great value for solo travelers, providing essential amenities at a lower cost.
- **Use Public Transportation Wisely:** Invest in a prepaid IC card like Suica or Pasmo for convenience and slight discounts on public transit. Consider regional passes if you're exploring areas outside of Tokyo.
- **Visit Free Attractions:** Japan is rich in natural beauty and historic sites that often have no entrance fee. Plan your itinerary to include

these gems.

- **Travel Off-Peak:** Avoiding travel during Japan's Golden Week, Obon Festival, and New Year can save you significantly on accommodation and transportation.

Total Suggested Budget for a 7-Day Trip & Tips on Gratuities: Planning a 7-day adventure in Japan requires a clear understanding of potential expenses to ensure a trip that's both memorable and financially manageable. Here, we'll break down a total suggested budget, including a segment on tips and gratuities, to help you navigate your journey with ease.

1. Accommodation: For a mix of budget to mid-range accommodations, budget approximately ¥50,000 to ¥140,000 ($370 to $1,036 USD) for the week.

2. Food: Averaging between budget meals and dining experiences, set aside about ¥49,000 to ¥70,000 ($362 to $517 USD) for the week.

3. Transportation: Including a 7-day Japan Rail Pass and local transportation, expect to spend around ¥35,000 to ¥50,000 ($259 to $370 USD).

4. Sightseeing: For various entry fees and special experiences, allocate approximately ¥14,000 to ¥35,000 ($103 to $259 USD).

5. Shopping and Souvenirs: Depending on your interests, ¥10,000 to ¥20,000 ($74 to $148 USD) should cover basic shopping desires.

Total Estimated Budget: ¥158,000 to ¥315,000 ($1,168 to $2,330 USD) for a 7-day trip. This range accommodates different travel styles, from economical to moderate spending, excluding international airfare.

Tips & Gratuities in General: In Japan, the culture around tipping differs significantly from many Western countries. Here are key points to remember:

- **Tipping is Not Customary:** In restaurants, hotels, and taxis, tipping is not a common practice. Service staff in Japan are paid a living wage, and excellent service is considered the standard, not something extra to be rewarded with tips.
- **Exceptions:** While tipping is generally not expected, there are a few exceptions. In high-end ryokan (traditional inns), it's customary to leave a small gratuity for the room attendant. This should be placed in a sealed envelope and given discreetly. The amount can vary, but ¥2,000 to ¥5,000 ($15 to $37 USD) is typical for a stay.
- **Guided Tours:** If you're taking a private tour and feel that your guide has provided exceptional service, a tip of ¥1,000 to ¥3,000 ($7 to $22 USD) is a kind gesture, though not obligatory. Ensure this is done discreetly and respectfully.

Weather

Japan's weather plays a pivotal role in shaping the experiences you can enjoy throughout the year. Each season brings its own unique charm, festivals, and activities, making any time a good time to visit, depending on what you're looking to experience. Here, we'll guide you through Japan's seasonal weather patterns, the best times to travel, and the activities and sights that make each season special.

Traveling through Japan offers a unique journey across its four distinct seasons, each brimming with its own set of celebrations, natural beauty, and activities that cater to every traveler's desires. As you plan your visit, understanding the weather patterns and seasonal highlights will enrich your experience, allowing you to fully immerse in the wonders of this diverse country.

Spring, stretching from March to May, is perhaps the most iconic season to visit Japan. It's when the cherry blossoms, or sakura, envelop the country in soft pinks and whites, creating a dreamlike atmosphere for hanami, the traditional cherry blossom viewing parties. The weather during this season is delightfully warm, with temperatures ranging from 10°C to 20°C (50°F to 68°F), offering perfect conditions for outdoor explorations. This period also hosts vibrant spring festivals, such as the Takayama Spring Festival, where you can witness Japan's rich cultural tapestry.

As the calendar turns to summer (June to August), the climate becomes hot and humid, with temperatures often soaring above 30°C (86°F). Despite the early summer's rainy season, the mood remains festive, highlighted by an array of festivals and fireworks displays. For those looking to escape the heat, the cooler, less humid regions of Hokkaido present an ideal retreat, with its beautiful landscapes and outdoor activities like Mount Fuji climbing, available only in July and August.

Autumn (September to November) ushers in a refreshing change with its comfortable temperatures (15°C to 25°C or 59°F to 77°F) and the spectacular changing colors of the leaves. It's a season that rivals spring in beauty, offering a palette of reds, oranges, and yellows across Japan's countryside and mountainous regions. Autumn not only invites koyo (autumn leaf) hunting in renowned spots like Kyoto and Nikko but also features unique seasonal festivals, including the Jidai Matsuri in Kyoto, celebrating Japan's historical periods.

Winter, from December to February, presents a stark contrast across

Japan. The northern areas, especially Hokkaido, are blanketed in snow, creating a winter wonderland perfect for skiing, snowboarding, and onsen visits against a snowy backdrop. Meanwhile, the southern regions, such as Okinawa, enjoy milder weather. This season is also marked by distinctive winter festivals, such as the Sapporo Snow Festival, showcasing spectacular ice and snow sculptures.

Choosing the best time for your visit depends on your interests: nature enthusiasts will find the spring and autumn seasons magical for their sakura and koyo views, respectively. Winter sports aficionados will revel in the snowy landscapes of Hokkaido or Nagano, ideal for skiing and snowboarding. Those drawn to cultural festivities will find summer and the transition seasons of spring and autumn filled with opportunities to engage in Japan's rich festival traditions. For travelers seeking milder weather and thinner crowds, the shoulder seasons of late spring and late autumn offer a tranquil atmosphere for city exploration and sightseeing. Each season in Japan unfolds with its unique charm and array of activities, ensuring that no matter when you choose to visit, your journey through this multifaceted country will be filled with memorable experiences, from its scenic vistas to its vibrant cultural celebrations.

What to Pack

Packing for a trip to Japan is an exercise in balancing essentials with the practicalities of travel across a country known for its varying climates, technological advancement, and cultural norms. Here's a comprehensive guide to help you pack smartly, ensuring you're well-prepared for everything from temple visits to tech-savvy cities, mountain retreats to bustling street markets.

Essentials for All Seasons

- **Passport and Documents:** Ensure your passport has sufficient validity (preferably six months beyond your stay) and organize all necessary visas. Carry a printed copy of your travel insurance and emergency contacts.
- **Cash and Cards:** While Japan is gradually becoming more card-friendly, cash is still king in many places. Carry a reasonable amount of yen, and inform your bank of your travel plans to avoid any card issues. A money belt or a secure way to carry your cash and cards is recommended for peace of mind.
- **Power Adapter and Portable Charger:** Japan uses Type A and B plugs, operating on a 100V supply voltage at 50/60Hz. A universal adapter and a reliable portable charger are indispensable for staying connected.
- **Comfortable Footwear:** Whether you're exploring ancient temples or navigating the urban sprawl, a pair of comfortable walking shoes is essential. Consider the season: breathable sneakers for warmer months and waterproof options for winter or the rainy season.

Clothing Essentials

- **Urban Exploration:** Pack smart-casual trousers or jeans for style and comfort, along with breathable, neatly tailored shirts or blouses suitable for transitioning from day to night. Don't forget a lightweight, stylish jacket or blazer for cooler evenings or visits to upscale venues, ensuring you're appropriately dressed for any urban adventure.
- **Temples and Traditional Sites:** When visiting temples and

traditional sites in Japan, choose modest outfits like long skirts, maxi dresses, or loose-fitting trousers that cover shoulders and knees. Opt for tops that provide adequate coverage and consider bringing a lightweight scarf or shawl for extra modesty or sun protection, ensuring respectfulness and comfort during your visits.

- **Outdoor Adventures:** For outdoor adventures in Japan, pack durable, moisture-wicking fabrics perfect for hiking and nature excursions. Include both short and long-sleeve shirts for versatile layering options. Comfortable hiking pants and a waterproof jacket are essential for protection against unpredictable weather. Lastly, don't forget quality hiking shoes with good grip to safely navigate varied terrains.

- **Seasonal Considerations:** For seasonal considerations, pack thermal tees, sweaters, and cardigans to accommodate fluctuating temperatures through easy layering. In summer, choose airy fabrics with UV protection, and don't forget a broad-brimmed hat, sunglasses, and sunscreen for sun safety. During winter, prepare with thermal undergarments, cozy sweaters, and a heavy coat, essential for the colder climates of northern regions and higher elevations.

- **General Essentials:** For general essentials, include comfortable, versatile shoes suited for extensive walking and appropriate for the season—waterproof for rainy months and breathable for summer. Also, pack socks since shoes are frequently removed in certain indoor settings in Japan.

Cultural Considerations and Miscellaneous

- **Respectful Attire:** When visiting temples or traditional establishments, modest dress is appreciated. A scarf or shawl can be handy for covering shoulders or legs when necessary.

- **Tech Gadgets:** Japan's tech landscape is vast. If you're a tech enthusiast, leave space in your bag for gadgets and gizmos you might pick up along the way. Often irresistible tech finds that are bound to catch your eye.
- **Medications and First Aid:** Bring any prescribed medications in their original containers, accompanied by your doctor's note. A basic first aid kit, with band-aids, pain relievers, and motion sickness tablets, can also be a lifesaver.
- **Language Guide or App:** While many Japanese people study English, communication can sometimes be challenging. A phrasebook or a translation app on your smartphone can help bridge the gap. Don't forget this book!
- **Eco-Friendly Items:** A reusable shopping bag, cutlery, and a water bottle can be very useful and help in reducing plastic waste, aligning with Japan's efforts towards sustainability.

Where to Stay

Choosing where to stay in Japan is a crucial part of planning your trip, as it can significantly impact your overall experience. Japan offers a wide range of accommodations to suit every preference and budget, from traditional ryokans and budget-friendly hostels to luxury hotels and unique capsule hotels. Here are some tips and essentials to consider when deciding where to stay in Japan.

Understanding the Options

Ryokans: These traditional Japanese inns offer a glimpse into Japan's cultural heritage, complete with tatami mat rooms, futon beds, and often, on-site onsen (hot springs). Staying in a ryokan is an experience in itself, ideal for those seeking to immerse themselves in Japanese traditions.

Hotels: Japan's hotels range from luxurious international chains to local business hotels offering compact, efficiently designed rooms at reasonable rates. Business hotels are a great option for travelers looking for comfort and convenience without the high price tag.

Hostels: For budget travelers and solo adventurers, hostels are an excellent choice. Many hostels in Japan are clean, modern, and offer both dormitory-style and private rooms, providing a social atmosphere and opportunities to meet fellow travelers.

Capsule Hotels: Perfect for a unique and economical stay, capsule hotels offer small, pod-like sleeping quarters with shared bathroom facilities. While space is limited, the experience is uniquely Japanese and perfect for those looking to maximize their time exploring.

Vacation Rentals: Platforms like Airbnb offer apartments and houses across Japan, providing a home-away-from-home experience. This option can be particularly cost-effective for groups or families and those planning longer stays.

Location Is Key

Proximity to Public Transportation: Japan's public transport system is world-renowned for its efficiency and coverage. Staying near a train or subway station can save you time and make it easier to explore.

Neighborhoods: Consider the vibe and attractions of different neighborhoods. For instance, Shibuya and Shinjuku in Tokyo are bustling with activity, while Kyoto's Gion district offers a more traditional atmosphere.

Booking Tips

Book in Advance: Accommodations, especially in peak seasons (cherry blossom season in spring and autumn foliage season), can fill up quickly. Booking several months in advance ensures more choices and often better rates.

Check Reviews: Online reviews can provide valuable insights into the cleanliness, service, and overall experience of staying at a particular place.

Consider Your Itinerary: Choose accommodations that align with your itinerary. If you plan to visit multiple cities, staying near major train stations can facilitate travel between destinations.

Cultural Etiquette

- **Respect the Rules:** Especially in traditional accommodations like ryokans, be mindful of etiquette rules, such as removing shoes at the entrance and respecting quiet hours.
- **Facility Usage:** Understand and respect the guidelines for using shared facilities, whether it's a hostel kitchen or a ryokan's onsen.

Transportation

Navigating Japan's transportation system is an adventure in efficiency and convenience. The country boasts an extensive network of trains, buses, and domestic flights, making it relatively easy to travel between cities and explore local areas. Here's a guide to help you understand and make the most of Japan's transportation options during your visit.

Trains

Japan Rail Pass (JR Pass): Ideal for tourists planning to travel between cities. JR Pass offers unlimited use, including the Shinkansen (bullet trains), for a set period (7, 14, or 21 days). It's cost-effective if you're planning multiple long-distance journeys but must be purchased outside of Japan before your trip.

Local and Regional Trains: For shorter, city-to-city or within-city travel, local and regional trains provide an efficient option. Tickets can be bought at station machines, and prepaid IC cards like Suica and Pasmo offer convenience for pay-as-you-go travel in and around urban areas.

Buses

Long-Distance Buses: A budget-friendly alternative to trains for intercity travel. Night buses are particularly popular for long distances, offering a way to save on one night's accommodation.

Local Buses: Useful for reaching destinations not covered by trains, though they can be more challenging to navigate due to less frequent English signage or announcements.

Domestic Flights

Air Travel: For covering large distances quickly, such as Tokyo to

Hokkaido or Okinawa, domestic flights can be time-saving. Low-cost carriers offer competitive prices, but always consider the travel time to and from airports.

Rental Cars and Bikes

Cars: In rural areas or for travelers wanting flexibility, renting a car is a viable option. Note that Japan drives on the left, an International Driving Permit (IDP) is required, and some areas have toll roads.

Bikes: Many cities, including Kyoto and Tokyo, are bike-friendly and offer rental services. Biking is an excellent way to explore at your own pace and can often be faster than navigating by public transport in urban centers.

Tips for Smooth Travel

- **Plan Ahead:** Use apps and websites like Hyperdia or Google Maps to plan routes and check schedules.
- **Rush Hour:** Try to avoid traveling during rush hour in major cities, as trains and subways can be incredibly crowded.
- **Reserved vs. Non-Reserved Seats:** On long-distance trains, including the Shinkansen, consider reserving seats for peace of mind, especially during peak travel times. Non-reserved cars are usually available but can get crowded.
- **Carry Cash:** While IC cards are widely accepted for public transport, having cash on hand is necessary for buses in more rural areas where IC cards might not be accepted.

How long to stay

Determining the ideal length for your Japan trip depends on what you want to do and see. For a broad cultural immersion or exploring multiple regions, plan for two to three weeks. If you're aiming to hit major cities like Tokyo, Kyoto, and Hiroshima, 7 to 10 days should be enough. Those with specific interests, such as festivals or culinary tours, might adjust their stay accordingly. Remember, traveling between different islands or rural areas takes time, so factor this into your plans. Keep in mind your budget and time constraints, and consider the efficiency of Japan's transport system to help manage your schedule and expenses. Lastly, leave some room for flexibility to explore unexpected finds or spend more time in places that captivate you.

3

Getting Settled Once You Arrive

Arriving in Japan, with its blend of tradition and cutting-edge modernity, can be exhilarating. This chapter aims to ease your transition, helping you get comfortably settled and acclimated to your new surroundings. From navigating transport to your accommodation to understanding the local customs and technology, we've got you covered.

Transport to Your Hotel/Airbnb

Trains: Direct train services like the Narita Express to Tokyo (around ¥3,000) and the Haruka to Kyoto from Kansai Airport (around ¥2,850) are efficient for city transfers. They're fast and have space for luggage. **Buses:** Airport limousine buses connect airports to major hotels and city areas, costing about ¥1,000 to ¥3,000, depending on the distance. They're convenient if your accommodation is near a bus stop. **Taxis:** Taxis provide door-to-door service but are pricier, with fares starting from ¥5,000, increasing with distance. Ideal for late arrivals or if you have lots of luggage. **Rental Cars:** Available at airports for those heading directly to rural areas. Prices vary widely based on the car and rental period. Remember, an international driving permit is required.

Using apps like Google Maps or Hyperdia can help navigate public transport options, showing routes, times, and costs. Choose based on your priorities, whether it's cost, convenience, or time.

Managing Jet Lag

- **Adjust Your Sleep Schedule:** Start shifting your sleep schedule a few days before departure to match Japan's time zone if possible.
- **Stay Hydrated:** Drink plenty of water before, during, and after your flight. Avoid alcohol and caffeine as they can exacerbate jet lag symptoms.
- **Seek Sunlight:** Once you arrive, expose yourself to natural sunlight during the day to help reset your internal clock.

- **Stay Active:** Engage in light exercise or walking to keep your energy up and improve your sleep quality at night.

Supermarket/Non-Restaurant Food Options

In Japan's main cities, such as Tokyo, Kyoto, and Osaka, you'll find plenty of affordable meal options at supermarkets and convenience stores.

- **Convenience Stores:** Chains like 7-Eleven, Lawson, and Family-Mart offer onigiri (rice balls), sandwiches, and bento boxes, with prices starting as low as ¥100 to ¥500. These stores are ubiquitous in city centers and residential areas alike.
- **Supermarkets:** Places like AEON, Seiyu, and local supermarkets provide a broader selection of fresh produce, snacks, and ready-to-eat meals. Look out for evening discounts on sushi and bento boxes, where prices drop to between ¥300 and ¥1,000 to clear daily stock.
- **100 Yen Shops:** Daiso and Seria are popular chains where you can pick up snacks, drinks, and basic groceries for ¥100. They're a great resource for travelers on a tight budget and can be found throughout major cities.

Wildlife to Expect

Japan's diverse ecosystems, ranging from its bustling urban centers to serene natural landscapes, are home to a fascinating array of wildlife. As you traverse the country, from the northern reaches of Hokkaido to the subtropical islands of Okinawa, here's what you might encounter.

Urban Wildlife: In cities such as Tokyo, Kyoto, and Osaka, beyond the typical urban birds like crows and sparrows, you might encounter more unique urban dwellers. Raccoons and tanuki (raccoon dogs) are often spotted in public parks and green spaces, adapting to city life. These animals are generally harmless but are best admired from a distance.

Sacred Deer: Nara Park in Nara and Miyajima Island near Hiroshima are famous for their freely roaming deer. Considered sacred in Shinto religion, these deer have become accustomed to human presence. Visitors can feed them special crackers sold in the area, but caution is advised as they can become assertive in their quest for treats.

Mountainous Wildlife: Japan's mountainous regions, such as the Japanese Alps, are home to a variety of animals. The snow monkeys of Jigokudani Monkey Park are a particular highlight, especially in winter when they bathe in the area's natural hot springs. These regions are also great for birdwatching, with species like the Japanese serow, a goat-antelope native to Japan, occasionally making an appearance.

Hokkaido's Unique Fauna: Hokkaido, Japan's northernmost island, offers wildlife experiences unlike any other part of the country. Here, you might see red-crowned cranes, known for their elegant courtship dances, and the Hokkaido deer. The island is also one of the few places in Japan where you can spot brown bears, primarily in Shiretoko National Park, a UNESCO World Heritage site.

Marine Life: Japan's extensive coastline and numerous islands offer rich marine biodiversity. In regions like Okinawa, snorkelers and divers can explore coral reefs teeming with colorful fish, sea turtles, and even manta rays. The coastal waters around the Izu Peninsula and in the Seto Inland Sea are also known for dolphin and whale-watching tours.

Insects and Butterflies: Japan's forests and rural areas are a haven for entomologists and nature enthusiasts, with a vast array of insects, including unique species of butterflies and the iconic Japanese rhinoceros beetle, especially during the summer months.

As you explore Japan, remember that while wildlife encounters can be a thrilling part of your experience, maintaining a respectful distance and not feeding wild animals (except where specifically allowed, such as in Nara) are important to preserve the natural behavior and habitat of these creatures. Whether you're navigating the urban jungle or venturing into the wild, Japan's wildlife adds a fascinating layer to the rich tapestry of experiences the country has to offer.

Nightlife to Expect

Japan's nightlife is as varied and vibrant as its day-time culture, offering something for every type of traveler. From the neon-lit streets of Tokyo's Shibuya and Shinjuku districts to the more subdued and traditional entertainment areas in Kyoto and Osaka, here's what you can look forward to.

Tokyo Nightlife: Tokyo is the heart of Japan's nightlife, with districts like Shibuya, Shinjuku, and Roppongi offering an array of options from high-energy nightclubs and bars to more relaxed izakayas (Japanese pubs) and karaoke rooms. Shibuya is famous for its youthful vibe and fashion, while Shinjuku's Kabukicho area is known for its entertainment and red-light district. Roppongi caters to a more international crowd, with many bars and clubs frequented by both locals and expats.

Osaka's Dotonbori: Osaka's nightlife centers around the Dotonbori area, known for its dazzling neon signs and street food vendors. It's a great place to experience the city's lively atmosphere, with ample opportunities to hop between izakayas, bars, and clubs. The Namba district is also popular for its nightlife, offering a mix of traditional and modern entertainment options.

Kyoto's Pontocho: Kyoto offers a more traditional nightlife experience. The Pontocho alleyway, running along the Kamo River, is lined with restaurants and bars in traditional wooden buildings, some of which offer dining with views of the river. Gion, Kyoto's famous geisha district, provides a unique glimpse into traditional Japanese entertainment, though experiencing a performance or dinner with a maiko (apprentice geisha) requires advance booking and can be quite expensive.

Hokkaido's Sapporo: In the north, Sapporo's Susukino district is renowned for its vibrant nightlife, with numerous bars, clubs, and restaurants catering to all tastes. It's particularly lively during the Sapporo Snow Festival in February.

Okinawa's Naha: For a tropical twist, Naha in Okinawa offers a laid-back nightlife scene with beach bars, live music venues featuring local and international artists, and izakayas serving Okinawan specialties.

Themed Bars and Cafes: Across Japan, themed bars and cafes offer unique experiences, from animal cafes (cat, owl, and hedgehog cafes) to establishments based on video games, movies, or traditional Japanese culture.

When enjoying Japan's nightlife, it's essential to respect local customs and regulations. Note that smoking is allowed in many bars and izakayas, and there's a legal drinking age of 20. With its wide range of options, Japan's nightlife scene offers memorable experiences for night owls and culture enthusiasts alike, providing a deeper understanding of the country's diverse entertainment landscape.

Customs and Culture to Expect

Japan's rich tapestry of customs and culture forms an integral part of its identity, distinguishing it as a destination that offers more than picturesque landscapes and advanced technology. For travelers, delving into these traditions is not merely about observing from the sidelines; it's about gaining a deeper appreciation and respect for the Japanese way of life. From the meticulous art of tea ceremonies that teach patience and mindfulness to the practice of omotenashi, which showcases Japan's unparalleled hospitality, understanding these customs enhances the travel experience. This cultural immersion allows travelers to engage with Japan on a meaningful level, transforming their journey into a truly enriching experience.

Here's what to expect and how to navigate these cultural nuances.

- **Respect and Politeness:** Japanese society places a high value on respect and politeness. Bowing is a common way to greet, thank, or apologize to someone. It's also polite to say "thank you" (arigatou) and "excuse me" (sumimasen) when interacting with locals.
- **Shoes Off:** It's customary to remove your shoes when entering someone's home, certain traditional accommodations like ryokans, temples, and even some restaurants. Slippers are often provided for indoor use.
- **Quiet Public Spaces:** Public transportation and public spaces often maintain a quiet atmosphere. Loud conversations, especially on trains and buses, are discouraged.
- **Cash is King:** Despite advancements in digital payment technologies, cash is still widely used, especially in smaller establishments and rural areas. Always carry some cash to avoid inconvenience.
- **Gift-Giving Culture:** Gift-giving is an important part of Japanese culture, emphasizing thoughtfulness and presentation. If visiting

someone or returning from travel, bringing a small gift (omiyage) is appreciated.

- **Dining Etiquette:** When dining, it's polite to say "itadakimasu" before eating and "gochisousama deshita" after finishing your meal as a way of showing gratitude. Remember not to stick your chopsticks vertically into a bowl of rice, as this resembles a funeral ritual.

- **Onsen Etiquette:** If visiting an onsen (hot spring), cleanliness is paramount. Bathe and rinse off thoroughly before entering the communal bath. Tattoos may be frowned upon in some onsens due to their association with the yakuza (Japanese mafia), though attitudes are slowly changing.

- **Conservative Dress:** While Japan's major cities are modern and fashion-forward, dressing conservatively, especially when visiting temples and shrines, is respectful. Avoid overly revealing clothing in these settings.

Sea Life to Expect

Japan's surrounding waters and diverse aquatic habitats are home to a rich variety of sea life, offering unique experiences for marine enthusiasts.

Coral Reefs in Okinawa: The subtropical climate of Okinawa hosts vibrant coral reefs teeming with colorful fish, sea turtles, and even manta rays, making it a prime spot for snorkeling and diving.

Coastal Waters: Japan's coastal areas, such as the Izu Peninsula and areas around the Seto Inland Sea, are known for dolphin and whale watching. Depending on the season, you might spot different species, including humpback and gray whales.

Aquariums: Japan boasts some world-class aquariums, like Okinawa Churaumi Aquarium and Osaka Aquarium Kaiyukan, where you can observe a wide range of marine life, from giant whale sharks to deep-sea creatures, in carefully recreated habitats.

Rivers and Lakes: Freshwater areas also host unique species. The iconic koi fish, often seen in temple ponds and traditional Japanese gardens, and the Japanese giant salamander, one of the world's largest amphibians, can be found in rivers across Japan.

Exploring Japan's sea life offers a glimpse into the country's commitment to preserving its natural heritage and provides opportunities for direct engagement with marine biodiversity. Whether diving into the crystal-clear waters of Okinawa or visiting one of the many aquariums, the marine world in Japan is sure to leave a lasting impression.

Technology to Expect

Japan is renowned for its technological advancements, and visitors will encounter a range of high-tech experiences.

- **High-Speed Internet:** Japan offers widespread access to high-speed internet, with free Wi-Fi available in many public areas, including train stations, cafes, and some city streets.
- **Advanced Toilets:** Japanese toilets, found in most hotels and public restrooms, feature heated seats, bidet functions, and sometimes even music or sound effects for privacy.
- **Vending Machines:** Ubiquitous across cities and rural areas, Japanese vending machines sell not just drinks and snacks but also items like umbrellas, electronics, and sometimes even fresh produce.
- **Public Transportation:** Japan's public transport system is a marvel of efficiency, with punctual trains, buses, and an extensive network of subway lines, especially in metropolitan areas like Tokyo and

Osaka.

- **Robotics and Automation:** In some restaurants and hotels, robots are used for tasks ranging from serving food to checking in guests, showcasing Japan's leadership in robotics.
- **Cashless Payments:** While cash is still widely used, cashless payment options are growing, with many places accepting IC cards, QR codes, and mobile payment apps.

Encountering Japan's technology can be one of the most fascinating aspects of visiting the country, reflecting its culture of innovation and convenience.

4

The Foods of Japan

Japanese cuisine offers a rich tapestry of flavors and experiences, from the simplicity of fresh sushi to the complexity of kaiseki, the traditional multi-course meal. This chapter delves into the must-try foods of Japan, exploring what each dish is and where to find the best examples across the country.

Sushi and Sashimi

What It Is: Sushi and sashimi stand at the heart of Japanese cuisine, representing its emphasis on freshness and simplicity. Sushi features vinegared rice paired with a variety of ingredients, including fresh fish, seafood, vegetables, and sometimes tropical fruits, presenting a harmonious blend of flavors and textures. Sashimi, by contrast, focuses purely on the art of thinly sliced raw fish or seafood, served without rice, allowing the natural flavors to shine through. This culinary art form is as much about the skill of the chef as it is about the quality of the ingredients, with the freshness of the fish being paramount.

Average Price: The cost of sushi and sashimi can vary widely depending on the type of establishment and the quality of ingredients. Mid-range sushi restaurants typically offer sets or individual pieces ranging from ¥2,000 to ¥10,000. For a more indulgent experience, premium sushi dining, including omakase (chef's selection) courses, can exceed ¥30,000 per person, reflecting the quality of the fish, the expertise of the chef, and the overall dining experience.

Best Places: Tokyo, as the epicenter of Japan's sushi culture, is home to some of the world's most renowned sushi restaurants. Tsukiji Market, although no longer the site of the famous tuna auction, remains a hub for fresh seafood and houses numerous sushi counters where visitors can enjoy sushi and sashimi made from the day's catch. Sushi Dai and Sushi Saito stand out for their exceptional offerings. Sushi Dai is known for its long queues and equally rewarding dining experience, offering some of the freshest sushi at reasonable prices. Sushi Saito, awarded three Michelin stars, is celebrated for its exquisite sushi and sashimi. Reservations are often required months in advance, underscoring the demand for this high-caliber dining experience.

Ramen

What It Is: Ramen is a quintessential Japanese dish that has gained international fame for its deep, rich flavors and comforting warmth. At its core, ramen consists of wheat noodles served in a savory broth, which can be flavored with miso, soy sauce (shoyu), salt (shio), or pork bone (tonkotsu). The dish is then topped with a variety of ingredients such as sliced pork (chashu), green onions, bamboo shoots (menma), seaweed (nori), and boiled eggs. The complexity of the broth, the chewiness of the noodles, and the quality of the toppings contribute to the uniqueness of each bowl.

Average Price: Ramen is known for its accessibility and affordability, making it a popular choice among locals and tourists alike. Prices typically range from ¥800 to ¥1,500 for a hearty bowl, with specialty and more elaborate bowls reaching up to ¥2,000. The price varies based on the restaurant's location, the ingredients used, and the complexity of the dish.

Best Places: Japan's ramen scene is incredibly diverse, with different regions boasting their own signature styles. Hakata, a district in Fukuoka City, is famed for its tonkotsu ramen, characterized by its rich, pork bone-based broth that's simmered for hours to achieve a creamy consistency. Notable spots in Hakata include Ichiran and Ippudo, where diners can customize the firmness of their noodles, the richness of the broth, and the level of spice. Sapporo, the capital of Hokkaido, is renowned for its miso ramen, a perfect dish to warm up during the cold winters. Ramen Yokocho and Ramen Kyowakoku are popular destinations in Sapporo for sampling various styles of miso ramen under one roof.

Kaiseki Ryori

What It Is: Kaiseki Ryori is the epitome of Japanese culinary tradition, a multi-course meal that emphasizes the natural flavors of seasonal ingredients through a variety of cooking techniques. Each course is meticulously prepared and beautifully presented, reflecting the current season in both taste and presentation. The meal typically includes an appetizer, sashimi, a simmered dish, a grilled dish, and a steamed course, among others, culminating in a seasonal dessert. Kaiseki is not just about the food but the overall dining experience, incorporating elements of Japanese aesthetics, art, and philosophy.

Average Price: The cost of a Kaiseki meal is a reflection of the quality of ingredients, the skill of the chef, and the overall dining experience. Prices usually range from ¥10,000 to ¥30,000, although high-end Kaiseki experiences, particularly in establishments that have earned

Michelin stars or similar accolades, can exceed ¥50,000 per person. The price reflects not just the meal itself but the ambiance, service, and the artistry involved in the preparation of each dish.

Best Places: Kyoto is considered the heart of Kaiseki cuisine due to its history as the former imperial capital and its abundance of high-quality, local ingredients. Restaurants like Kikunoi and Kitcho are iconic, offering exquisite Kaiseki experiences that are deeply rooted in Kyoto's culinary traditions. Kikunoi, under the guidance of Chef Yoshihiro Murata, offers a menu that changes monthly to reflect the freshest seasonal ingredients, while Kitcho, renowned for its artful presentation and impeccable service, provides a dining experience that many consider a once-in-a-lifetime opportunity. Both restaurants require reservations well in advance and offer private dining rooms overlooking traditional Japanese gardens, enhancing the sensory experience of the meal.

Fugu (Pufferfish)

What It Is: Fugu, or pufferfish, is one of Japan's most notorious delicacies, celebrated for its unique texture and subtle flavor. The intrigue surrounding fugu comes from its potential lethality; the fish contains tetrodotoxin, a potent poison, in its organs. As a result, chefs must undergo rigorous training and certification to prepare fugu safely. The dish is served in various forms, including sashimi (thinly sliced), nabe (hot pot), and even fugu fin sake (hirezake), where the grilled fin is steeped in hot sake.

Average Price: The cost of indulging in fugu varies widely, typically ranging from ¥5,000 to ¥30,000. The price is influenced by the type of dish, the restaurant's prestige, and the season, as fugu is considered to be at its best during the colder months from October to March.

Best Places: Shimonoseki, located at the westernmost tip of Honshu, is renowned as Japan's fugu capital. The city's proximity to the rich fishing grounds of the Kanmon Straits ensures a steady supply of fresh fugu, and it hosts numerous specialty restaurants. Tokyo and Osaka also boast a selection of reputable fugu restaurants, with Zuboraya in Osaka being particularly famous. Zuboraya is easily recognizable by its iconic pufferfish lantern hanging outside and offers a range of fugu dishes in a welcoming atmosphere, making it a great introduction to this unique culinary experience.

Okonomiyaki

What It Is: Okonomiyaki is a beloved Japanese comfort food often described as a savory pancake, made from a batter mixed with cabbage and a variety of other ingredients such as seafood, pork, and green onions. The name "okonomiyaki" literally means "as you like it," reflecting the dish's versatility. It's cooked on a griddle and typically topped with okonomiyaki sauce, mayonnaise, dried seaweed (aonori), and bonito flakes, creating a rich blend of flavors and textures.

Average Price: This accessible and satisfying meal is budget-friendly, with prices usually ranging from ¥700 to ¥1,500 per pancake. The cost may vary based on the size and choice of ingredients.

Best Places: Okonomiyaki has two main regional variations: Hiroshima-style, where ingredients are layered, and Osaka-style, in which all ingredients are mixed together before cooking. Hiroshima's Okonomimura, a multi-story complex dedicated to the dish, offers visitors the chance to explore numerous stalls each putting their unique spin on Hiroshima-style okonomiyaki. In Osaka, Fukutaro is a well-regarded establishment known for its flavorful Osaka-style okonomiyaki, showcasing why the city is often called the nation's kitchen.

Unagi no Kabayaki

What It Is: Unagi no Kabayaki is a classic Japanese dish featuring freshwater eel grilled to perfection and basted with a sweet soy-based sauce. The eel is first skewered, then grilled, and finally coated in the sauce, which caramelizes upon the eel's surface, offering a delightful mix of smoky and sweet flavors. This dish is not only cherished for its taste but also for its supposed stamina-boosting properties, making it especially popular during the hot summer months.

Average Price: The cost of enjoying Unagi no Kabayaki can range from ¥2,000 to ¥4,000. Prices vary depending on the establishment's location, the size of the serving, and the quality of the eel. During the peak season of unagi, prices might be on the higher end due to increased demand.

Best Places: Narita is renowned for its unagi dishes, with restaurants like Kawatoyo offering a memorable dining experience where guests can watch as the eel is expertly prepared and grilled. Hamamatsu in Shizuoka Prefecture is another hotspot for unagi, known for its high-quality eels and traditional preparation methods. Both cities pride themselves on their unagi cuisine, drawing food enthusiasts from across Japan and around the world.

Wagyu Beef

What It Is: Wagyu beef, known for its exceptional marbling, tenderness, and rich flavor, represents the pinnacle of Japanese beef quality. The term "Wagyu" translates to "Japanese cow" and encompasses several breeds, including the famed Kobe beef, which comes from the Tajima strain of Wagyu cattle. This beef is celebrated for its high degree of marbling, which provides a melt-in-your-mouth texture and a deep, complex flavor.

Average Price: The cost of Wagyu beef can vary significantly, from ¥5,000 to ¥30,000, depending on the cut, grade, and restaurant. Premium cuts and higher grades of Wagyu, such as A5, the highest grade based on marbling, color, brightness, and quality of fat, can fetch prices at the upper end of this range.

Best Places: Kobe is synonymous with high-quality Wagyu beef, offering authentic experiences in restaurants throughout the city. Tokyo, as a culinary capital, also boasts a wide array of establishments serving top-grade Wagyu, with Seryna being a notable example. Seryna specializes in Sukiyaki and Shabu Shabu, traditional Japanese hot pot dishes that highlight the delicate flavor and texture of Wagyu beef.

Chanko Nabe

What It Is: Chanko Nabe is a robust, nourishing stew closely tied to Japan's sumo wrestling tradition. It's a calorie-dense meal designed to help sumo wrestlers gain weight, consisting of a rich broth filled with a hearty mix of meat, fish, tofu, and vegetables. The ingredients vary widely but always aim to provide a balanced, high-calorie meal. Chanko Nabe is not just for sumo wrestlers; it's become a popular dish among locals and tourists alike for its satisfying, comforting qualities.

Average Price: Enjoying a bowl of Chanko Nabe typically costs between ¥2,000 and ¥3,000 per person. This price can vary based on the restaurant's location and the variety of ingredients used in the stew.

Best Places: The Ryogoku district in Tokyo, often considered the heart of the sumo world, is the best place to experience authentic Chanko Nabe. Here, restaurants like Chanko Tomoegata, often run by retired sumo wrestlers, serve up this hearty dish in an atmosphere filled with sumo memorabilia, offering diners a taste of sumo culture alongside their meal.

Hokkaido Seafood

What It Is: Hokkaido, Japan's northernmost prefecture, is surrounded by the cold waters of the North Pacific, making it an ideal location for some of the freshest and most diverse seafood in the country. Renowned for its crab, scallops, sea urchin, and salmon, Hokkaido's seafood is a must-try for any visitor to the region. The quality and variety of seafood available here are unparalleled, with the cold sea waters contributing to the rich flavors and textures.

Average Price: The cost of Hokkaido seafood can range from ¥2,000 to ¥10,000, largely depending on the type of seafood, the preparation, and where you choose to enjoy it. Fresh crab and high-grade sea urchin, for example, can be on the higher end of the price spectrum.

Best Places: Sapporo, the capital city of Hokkaido, offers numerous spots to savor the local seafood. Nijo Market, a bustling seafood market in the heart of Sapporo, allows visitors to sample a wide array of seafood, either raw or cooked, in a lively atmosphere. For those specifically seeking crab, Kani Honke in Sapporo is a renowned restaurant specializing in crab dishes, serving everything from whole grilled crab to crab hot pots.

Yuba

What It Is: Yuba, often referred to as tofu skin, is a delicate and flavorful Japanese delicacy made from the skin that forms on the surface of boiling soy milk. Esteemed for its subtle taste and versatile texture, yuba can be enjoyed in various forms – fresh, dried, or as an ingredient in soups, salads, and even sushi. Its gentle, slightly nutty flavor makes it a favorite in vegetarian cuisine, embodying the essence of simplicity and purity in Japanese cooking.

Average Price: Yuba dishes, particularly when part of a set meal, range in price from ¥1,500 to ¥3,000. The cost reflects not just the yuba itself but the craftsmanship involved in its preparation and the quality of the accompanying dishes.

Best Places: Kyoto is renowned for its yuba, thanks in part to the city's rich Zen Buddhist history and its emphasis on shojin ryori (Buddhist vegetarian cuisine). The area around Kyoto's temples, such as those in the Higashiyama district, is dotted with restaurants and cafes that specialize in yuba dishes, offering a serene dining experience that connects diners with the city's spiritual and culinary heritage.

Matcha Desserts

What It Is: Matcha desserts incorporate matcha, a finely ground powder made from specially grown and processed green tea leaves, known for its vibrant green color and distinct, slightly bitter flavor. In Japan, matcha is not only a ceremonial drink but also a popular ingredient in sweets and desserts, ranging from ice cream and cakes to traditional Japanese wagashi (sweets) like mochi and dorayaki.

Average Price: Prices for matcha desserts can vary widely, typically ranging from ¥300 for a simple matcha ice cream cone to ¥1,500 for more elaborate dessert creations in cafes or specialty dessert shops.

Best Places: Kyoto, the heart of Japan's tea culture, is renowned for its matcha and matcha desserts. Traditional tea houses and modern cafes alike offer a wide array of matcha-flavored treats. Tokyo also boasts a vibrant scene for matcha desserts, with places like Nakamura Tokichi and Tsujiri offering a modern take on matcha sweets. Additionally, Uji, a city near Kyoto, is famous for its high-quality matcha and is home to numerous shops specializing in matcha desserts.

Navigating Japan's culinary scene introduces you to the country's rich cultural heritage and regional specialties. From the high-end delicacy of fugu to the comforting simplicity of a bowl of ramen, each dish offers a window into the diverse flavors and traditions of Japan. Whether you're dining in a bustling city market or a serene, traditional ryokan, the food of Japan promises to be a highlight of your travels.

5

Best Restaurants in Japan

Japan's culinary landscape is as diverse as it is exquisite, with each city offering its own unique dining experiences. From the world-renowned sushi counters of Tokyo to the historic tofu restaurants of Kyoto, here's a guide to some of the best restaurants across Japan, highlighting their signature dishes, price range, and what makes them stand out.

Tokyo

Sukiyabashi Jiro: Famed from the documentary "Jiro Dreams of Sushi," this Michelin-starred restaurant offers an unparalleled sushi experience, led by sushi master Jiro Ono.
  - **Signature Dish:** Omakase sushi course.
  - **Price Range:** Over ¥30,000.
  - Reservations are required well in advance, and the experience is both exclusive and costly.

Obana: Known for its unagi (eel) dishes.
  - **Signature Dish:** Unaju (grilled eel over rice).

- **Price Range:** ¥3,000 to ¥5,000.
- Obana offers a traditional dining experience focused on a Japanese delicacy.

Ryugin: A modern take on kaiseki cuisine that incorporates innovative techniques.
- **Signature Dish:** Seasonal kaiseki course.
- **Price Range:** ¥20,000 to ¥30,000.
- Reservations are necessary for this Michelin-starred experience.

Yakitori Hachibei: Specializes in yakitori (grilled chicken skewers).
- **Signature Dish:** Assorted yakitori skewers.
- **Price Range:** ¥2,000 to ¥4,000.
- A more casual yet authentic dining option.

Kyoto

Kikunoi: Offers exquisite kaiseki dining.
- **Signature Dish:** Seasonal kaiseki course.
- **Price Range:** ¥10,000 to ¥30,000.
- A culinary journey through Kyoto's seasons.

Tofu Ryori Sasanoyuki: Specializes in tofu dishes.
- **Signature Dish:** Tofu kaiseki.
- **Price Range:** ¥3,000 to ¥5,000.
- A must-visit for vegetarian and tofu lovers.

Kappo Sakamoto: Known for its refined Japanese cuisine.
- **Signature Dish:** Seasonal fish dishes.
- **Price Range:** ¥8,000 to ¥15,000.
- A blend of traditional and modern kappo dining.

Omen: Famous for its udon noodles.
  - **Signature Dish:** Udon with various toppings.
  - **Price Range:** ¥1,000 to ¥2,000.
  - A casual spot for noodle enthusiasts.

Takase: Renowned for its kaiseki meals in a tranquil setting.
  - **Signature Dish:** Seasonal kaiseki course.
  - **Price Range:** ¥15,000 to ¥25,000.
  - Offers a peaceful dining experience near the Kamogawa River.

Osaka

Dotonbori Kukuru: Best known for takoyaki (octopus balls).
  - **Signature Dish:** Takoyaki.
  - **Price Range:** ¥500 to ¥1,000.
  - Perfect for a quick, flavorful snack.

Fujiya 1935: A contemporary take on Japanese cuisine.
  - **Signature Dish:** Seasonal tasting menu.
  - **Price Range:** ¥10,000 to ¥20,000.
  - A Michelin-starred dining experience that blends international techniques with local ingredients.

Tamajima: Specializes in egg-based dishes.
  - **Signature Dish:** Tamago kake gohan (egg over rice).
  - **Price Range:** ¥1,000 to ¥2,000.
  - A cozy spot offering comfort food.

Hokkaido, Sapporo

Kani-Honke: Celebrated for its crab dishes.

- **Signature Dish:** Crab kaiseki.
- **Price Range:** ¥5,000 to ¥10,000.
- A must-visit for seafood lovers.

Ramen Shingen: Known for its miso ramen.
- **Signature Dish:** Miso ramen.
- **Price Range:** ¥800 to ¥1,200.
- Offers a taste of Hokkaido's famous ramen.

Fukuoka

Ichiran: Specializes in tonkotsu ramen.
- **Signature Dish:** Customizable tonkotsu ramen.
- **Price Range:** ¥800 to ¥1,000.
- Known for its individual dining booths.

Tempura Hirao: Famous for its tempura.
- **Signature Dish:** Tempura set meal.
- **Price Range:** ¥2,000 to ¥4,000.
- Offers a crispy, light take on this classic dish.

Nara

Maguro Koya: Renowned for its tuna dishes.
- **Signature Dish:** Tuna steak.
- **Price Range:** ¥2,000 to ¥4,000.
- A small, intimate dining experience.

Nakatanidou: Famous for its mochi.
- **Signature Dish:** Yomogi mochi.
- **Price Range:** ¥200 to ¥500.

- Watch mochi being made in a thrilling performance.

Soba Sasuga: Specializes in soba noodles.
- **Signature Dish:** Cold soba with dipping sauce.
- **Price Range:** ¥1,000 to ¥2,000.
- A refreshing, authentic noodle experience.

Kanazawa

Sushi Ippei: Offers an intimate sushi dining experience.
- **Signature Dish:** Omakase sushi course.
- **Price Range:** ¥10,000 to ¥20,000.
- Known for its fresh, local seafood.

Tsubajin: Renowned for its traditional kaiseki meals.
- **Signature Dish:** Seasonal kaiseki course.
- **Price Range:** ¥10,000 to ¥15,000.
- A dining experience in a historic setting.

Each of these restaurants offers a glimpse into Japan's rich culinary heritage, from street food to high-end dining. Whether you're seeking the comfort of a steaming bowl of ramen or the refined elegance of kaiseki, Japan's dining scene caters to every palate and budget.

6

Secret Spots

Japan, a land of profound natural beauty and deep cultural heritage, holds many secrets waiting to be discovered by those willing to step off the beaten path. Beyond the bustling streets of Tokyo and the historic temples of Kyoto lies a world of hidden gems that offer a glimpse into the country's unique blend of natural wonders, historical depth, and cultural richness. From the thatched-roof villages nestled in the mountains to secluded islands shrouded in mystery, and from ancient trails through timeless forests to serene onsens in snow-covered landscapes, these secret spots invite adventurers and culture enthusiasts alike to explore Japan's lesser-known facets. This chapter aims to guide you through some of Japan's most enchanting hidden treasures, providing details on their locations, what makes them special, parking information, and other useful tips to enhance your journey. These destinations promise experiences filled with natural beauty, historical intrigue, and cultural authenticity, making them well worth the visit for those looking to delve deeper into the heart of Japan.

The Village of Shirakawa-go

Located in Gifu Prefecture's mountains, Shirakawa-go is a UNESCO World Heritage site famous for its gassho-zukuri farmhouses with steep thatched roofs designed for heavy snow. Accessible from Takayama or Kanazawa, this village is a living museum showcasing traditional Japanese rural life and architecture.

Location: Access via bus from Takayama or Kanazawa.

Special Features: Gassho-zukuri farmhouses, traditional lifestyle, picturesque landscapes.

Parking and Expenses: Parking available near the village entrance, costing ¥500 to ¥1,000. Activities and experiences range from ¥500 to ¥2,000. Additional costs for dining and souvenirs.

Advice:

- Visit in winter for snow-covered scenery or during spring and autumn for vibrant landscapes.
- Consider an overnight stay in a farmhouse guesthouse (minshuku) for a full experience.
- Village exploration is best on foot; prepare for weather changes.
- Respect the community by observing private property and local guidelines.

Tomogashima Islands

The Tomogashima Islands, located in the Seto Inland Sea near Wakayama City, are a group of islands known for their historical military ruins and natural beauty. Once used for military fortifications, the islands now attract visitors for their unique blend of history and nature.

Location: Accessible by ferry from Kada Port in Wakayama City.

Special Features: Historical military ruins, hiking trails, untouched natural landscapes.

Parking and Expenses: Parking available at Kada Port; fees vary. The ferry to the islands costs around ¥2,000 round trip. There are minimal expenses on the islands themselves but bring cash for the ferry and any snacks.

Advice:

- Best visited during daylight hours for safety and to fully enjoy the sights.
- Wear comfortable shoes for hiking and exploring the ruins.
- Limited facilities on the islands; bring water and food.
- Check ferry times in advance to ensure a return trip.

The Sand Dunes of Tottori (Tottori Sakyu)

The Tottori Sand Dunes are the largest sand dunes in Japan, offering a unique landscape that contrasts dramatically with the country's typically lush scenery. Located near Tottori City on the coast of the Sea of Japan, these dunes provide visitors with a desert-like experience, complete with camel rides and sandboarding.

Location: A short bus ride from Tottori Station.

Special Features: Vast sand dunes, activities like camel rides (around ¥1,300) and sandboarding.

Parking and Expenses: Parking available near the dunes, with a small fee (around ¥500). Activities such as camel rides and sandboarding have separate charges.

Advice:

- Early morning or late afternoon visits offer the best light for photos and cooler temperatures.
- Wear appropriate footwear for sand and bring sun protection.
- Check weather conditions, as the area can be windy.

Kiso Valley

Kiso Valley, known for its preserved post towns like Magome and Tsumago along the historic Nakasendo trail, offers a glimpse into Japan's Edo period. Nestled in the Nagano Prefecture, this area is celebrated for its scenic beauty and historical significance.

Location: Accessible by train and bus combinations from Nagoya or

Matsumoto.

Special Features: Well-preserved Edo period post towns, hiking opportunities along the Nakasendo trail.

Parking and Expenses: Limited parking available in the post towns, often free or for a nominal fee. Hiking the trail is free, but some transportation between towns (like bus or taxi) may incur costs.

Advice:

- Plan to walk part of the Nakasendo trail for the full experience; it's suitable for most fitness levels.
- Stay overnight in a traditional inn (ryokan) to immerse yourself fully in the area's historical ambiance.
- Visit local eateries to try regional specialties like soba noodles.

Yakushima Island

Yakushima Island, a UNESCO World Heritage site, is celebrated for its ancient cedar forests, including the iconic Jomon Sugi, and diverse ecosystems. Located south of Kyushu, it's a paradise for nature lovers and hikers.

Location: Accessible by ferry or plane from Kagoshima.

Special Features: Ancient cedar trees, hiking trails, hot springs, and waterfalls.

Parking and Expenses: Some trailheads have parking, usually free. Entrance to the island and hiking is free, but transportation on the island (rental cars, buses) and accommodations vary in price. Expect to spend for activities like guided tours or hot springs entry.

Advice:

- Weather can change rapidly; bring appropriate gear for rain and varying temperatures.
- Booking accommodations in advance is recommended, especially during peak seasons.
- Respect the natural environment by staying on trails and taking all trash with you.

Aogashima Island

Aogashima Island, a volcanic island in the Philippine Sea, is part of the Izu Islands chain. Known for its unique geological formations and tranquil, remote atmosphere, it's one of Japan's most secluded and intriguing destinations.

Location: Accessible by helicopter or boat from Tokyo, with services more frequently available from Hachijojima Island.

Special Features: Volcanic crater, hot springs, hiking trails, and star-gazing opportunities.

Parking and Expenses: Limited need for parking due to the island's small size and remote nature. Travel to the island can be costly, with helicopter flights and boat rides varying in price (approximately ¥10,000 to ¥20,000 one way from Hachijojima). Minimal expenses on the island itself, but accommodation and food should be budgeted for.

Advice:

- Plan carefully, as weather can affect transportation to and from the island.
- Stay at least a couple of nights to experience the island's natural beauty fully and to account for possible travel delays.
- Bring cash, as ATM and card services may be limited.

Shimanami Kaido

Shimanami Kaido is a scenic toll road that spans the Seto Inland Sea, connecting Japan's main island of Honshu to the island of Shikoku via a series of bridges and islands. It's renowned for its breathtaking views and is a popular route for cycling enthusiasts.

Location: The route starts in Onomichi City, Hiroshima Prefecture, and ends in Imabari City, Ehime Prefecture.

Special Features: Cycling paths, beautiful sea and island views, and access to small islands along the route.

Parking and Expenses: Parking available at both ends of the route and on some of the islands. Bicycle rental services range from ¥1,000 to ¥3,000 per day. The toll for cyclists is about ¥500 to cross all bridges, making it an affordable adventure.

Advice:

- Consider renting a bicycle at one end and returning it at the other to fully enjoy the route.
- Plan for stops along the way to explore the islands' attractions, including temples, beaches, and local eateries.
- Stay hydrated and wear sunscreen, especially during summer months.

Shimanami Kaido offers a unique way to experience the beauty of the Seto Inland Sea and its islands, ideal for cyclists and travelers looking for a leisurely adventure through one of Japan's most picturesque regions.

Zao Fox Village

Zao Fox Village, located near Shiroishi in Miyagi Prefecture, is a unique animal sanctuary that is home to over a hundred free-roaming foxes, along with other animals. It's a must-visit for wildlife enthusiasts and those looking to experience a different side of Japan.

Location: Accessible by train and bus from Sendai, followed by a short taxi ride.

Special Features: Interaction with various types of foxes in a semi-wild setting, opportunities to feed the foxes, and seasonal views of the surrounding Zao Mountains.

Parking and Expenses: Parking is available on-site for visitors driving to the village. Entrance fee is about ¥1,000 per person, with additional costs for fox food and souvenirs.

Advice:

- Feeding foxes is allowed only in designated areas with food purchased from the village.
- Exercise caution and follow the village's guidelines to ensure a safe visit for both you and the animals.
- Visit during the feeding times for a more interactive experience

Wisteria Tunnel at Kawachi Fuji Gardens

The Wisteria Tunnel at Kawachi Fuji Gardens, located in Kitakyushu, Fukuoka Prefecture, is a breathtakingly beautiful passage adorned with cascading wisteria flowers. It's especially popular during the blooming season in late April to mid-May, attracting visitors from around the world.

Location: Accessible by bus or car from Kitakyushu City.

Special Features: Vibrant wisteria blooms forming a stunning floral tunnel, various types of wisteria in different colors, and the garden's picturesque landscape.

Parking and Expenses: Parking is available near the gardens. Entrance fees range from ¥500 to ¥1,500, depending on the bloom's peak season. Advance reservations may be required during peak bloom periods.

Advice:

- Plan your visit during the early morning or late afternoon to avoid crowds and to experience the best light for photography.
- Check the garden's official website or social media for updates on the blooming condition before your visit.
- Be respectful of the gardens and follow all posted guidelines to help preserve the beauty of the wisteria tunnel for future visitors.

Ginzan Onsen

Ginzan Onsen is a picturesque hot spring town nestled in the mountains of Yamagata Prefecture. Known for its nostalgic atmosphere, reminiscent of Japan's Taisho Era, its traditional ryokan (Japanese inns) lining a quaint cobblestone street create a serene retreat perfect for relaxation.

Location: Accessible by bus from Oishida Station, which is reached by train from Yamagata City.

Special Features: Historical ryokans, outdoor public baths, and a charming setting enhanced by the seasonal beauty of the surrounding nature.

Parking and Expenses: Limited parking available at some ryokans for guests. Staying overnight at a ryokan ranges from ¥15,000 to ¥30,000 per person, including two meals and onsen access. Day visitors can use public baths for about ¥500 to ¥1,000.

Advice:

- Book your stay in advance, especially during peak seasons like winter and autumn, to secure accommodation.
- Explore the town in the evening when the street and buildings are beautifully illuminated.

- Remember to bring cash, as some smaller establishments may not accept credit cards.

As you plan your journey, remember to embrace the spirit of adventure, respect the natural and cultural environments you explore, and cherish the memories made in Japan's hidden corners.

7

Top Attractions

Ancient traditions intermingle with futuristic innovation, offers an array of attractions that cater to every type of traveler. From the historic temples and shrines that whisper tales of the past to the neon-lit streets of Tokyo that showcase the pinnacle of modernity, Japan's top attractions provide a window into the soul of this unique country. Here's a guide to some of Japan's must-visit sites, their locations, what makes them special, along with practical information to enhance your visit.

Traditional Attractions

Japan's rich history and cultural heritage are showcased through its traditional attractions, including temples and shrines, castles, and historic towns. These sites offer a glimpse into the country's past, from its spiritual practices to its feudal history.

Temples and Shrines

Description: Temples and shrines are integral to Japanese culture, providing spaces for worship and community gatherings. Temples are Buddhist, while shrines are Shinto. **Locations:** Kyoto's Kinkaku-ji (Golden Pavilion) and Tokyo's Senso-ji. Kyoto, Nara, and Ise are renowned for their historic and spiritual significance. **Activities:** Participate in rituals, observe traditional architecture, and enjoy serene gardens. **Parking:** Varies by location; major sites often have nearby parking, but public transport is recommended. **Cost:** Many temples and shrines are free to enter, though some may charge a small fee (¥300 to ¥1,000) for entering specific buildings or gardens. **Advice:** Respect the religious and cultural practices. Photography may be restricted in sacred areas.

Castles

Description: Japanese castles are architectural marvels that served as fortresses and residences for feudal lords. Their design reflects strategic defense needs and aesthetic considerations. **Locations:** Himeji Castle, a UNESCO World Heritage site, and Matsumoto Castle are among the most famous. **Activities:** Explore castle grounds, towers, and museums to learn about samurai culture. **Parking:** Available at or near most castles. Fees vary. **Cost:** Entrance fees range from ¥500 to ¥1,500. **Advice:** Wear comfortable shoes for walking and climbing steep stairs. Check for renovation schedules to avoid disappointment.

Historic Towns

Description: Historic towns in Japan have preserved the look and feel of bygone eras, with traditional wooden buildings, teahouses, and sometimes even samurai residences. **Locations:** Kanazawa's Higashi Chaya District, Takayama's Sanmachi Suji, and the post towns of the Nakasendo trail, like Magome and Tsumago. **Activities:** Stroll through old streets, visit museums and craft shops, and enjoy local cuisine. **Parking:** Public parking areas are available, but spaces can be limited. Exploring by foot or public transport is often easier. **Cost:** Exploring the towns is generally free, but some museums and historical houses may charge admission fees (¥300 to ¥1,000). **Advice:** Respect local residents' privacy. Many of these towns offer ryokan stays for a full immersive experience.

These traditional attractions offer not just a journey through Japan's history but also a deeper understanding of its cultural roots, making them essential visits for anyone looking to experience the country's rich heritage.

Technology and Modern Attractions

Japan's embrace of the future is visible in its technological innovations and modern attractions. From the neon-lit streets of Tokyo's Akihabara to the cutting-edge art installations of TeamLab Borderless, these destinations provide a glimpse into the country's forward-thinking mindset.

Tokyo's Akihabara District

Description: Akihabara is the heart of Japan's otaku culture, known for its electronic stores, anime and manga shops, and maid cafes. **Location:** Central Tokyo **Activities:** Shop for electronics, anime merchandise, and experience themed cafes. **Parking:** Limited; public transport is recommended. **Cost:** Free to explore; costs vary for purchases and cafe visits. **Advice:** Be prepared for crowded streets and a sensory overload of sights and sounds.

Robot Restaurant

Description: A flashy entertainment venue in Tokyo's Shinjuku, known for its robot-themed performances. **Location:** Shinjuku, Tokyo **Activities:** Watch high-energy robot battles and neon-lit dancers. **Parking:** Limited; public transport is recommended. **Cost:** Around ¥8,000 for a show, excluding meals. **Advice:** Book in advance and be ready for a loud, lively experience.

TeamLab Borderless

Description: An immersive digital art museum that blurs the boundaries between art and technology. **Location:** Odaiba, Tokyo **Activities:** Explore interactive, digital art installations spread across vast, darkened spaces. **Parking:** Available in Odaiba. **Cost:** ¥3,200 for adults; discounts for children and seniors. **Advice:**Buy tickets in advance; wear comfortable shoes as you'll be walking a lot.

Miraikan (National Museum of Emerging Science and Innovation)

Description: A museum dedicated to showcasing advancements in science and technology, including space exploration and robotics. **Location:** Odaiba, Tokyo **Activities:** Interactive exhibits, ASIMO robot demonstrations, and a planetarium. **Parking:** Available in Odaiba. **Cost:** ¥620 for adults; free for children under 18. **Advice:** Check the schedule for live demonstrations and talks.

Nintendo Tokyo and Pokémon Centers

Description: Retail stores offering a vast selection of Nintendo and Pokémon merchandise, including exclusive items. **Location:** Shibuya (Nintendo Tokyo) and various locations for Pokémon Centers. **Activities:**Shopping for games, toys, and collectibles. **Parking:** Available at shopping centers but can be expensive. **Cost:** Free to enter; product costs vary. **Advice:** Weekdays are less crowded than weekends.

Toyota Commemorative Museum of Industry and Technology

Description: A museum in Nagoya showcasing Toyota's history and innovations in automotive technology. **Location:** Nagoya **Activities:** Explore the evolution of cars and textile machinery. **Parking:** Available on-site. **Cost:** ¥500 for adults; discounts for students and children. **Advice:** Allow several hours to fully enjoy the exhibits.

Roppongi Hills Mori Tower (Mori Art Museum and Tokyo City View)

Description: A mixed-use skyscraper in Tokyo offering art exhibitions and panoramic city views. **Location:**Roppongi, Tokyo **Activities:** Visit the Mori Art Museum and the observation deck. **Parking:** Available in Roppongi Hills. **Cost:** ¥1,800 for the museum and observation deck. **Advice:** Visit near sunset for spectacular views of Tokyo.

High-speed Trains (Shinkansen)

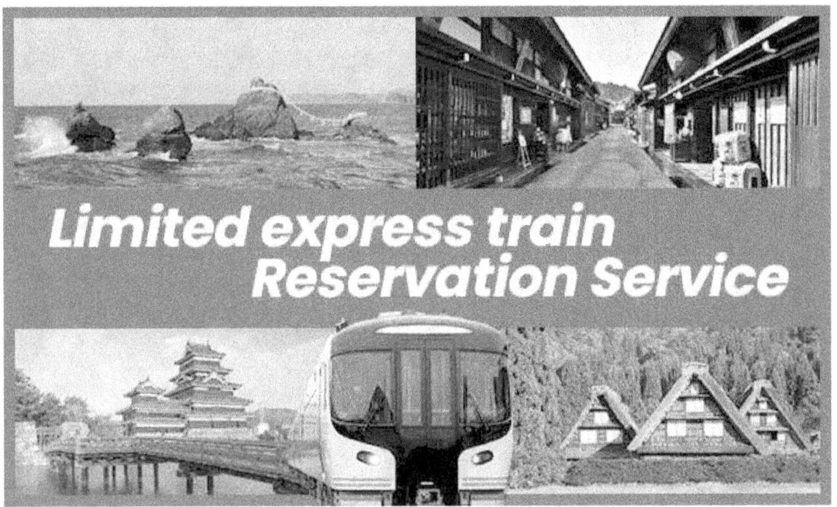

Description: Japan's bullet trains, known for their speed, efficiency, and comfort, connecting major cities across the country. **Location:** Nationwide **Activities:** Experience traveling at speeds of up to 320 km/h.**Parking:** At train stations but using public transport to reach them is recommended. **Cost:** Varies by distance; Tokyo to Kyoto costs around ¥13,000 one-way. **Advice:** Reserve seats in advance, especially during holiday periods.

These modern attractions and technological marvels offer a glimpse into Japan's innovative spirit and are a testament to its status as a leader in the fusion of tradition with futuristic advancement. Whether you're exploring the electric buzz of Akihabara or marveling at the efficiency of the Shinkansen, Japan's modern side is as enriching as its historical roots.

8

Day Trips

This chapter is designed to guide you through some meticulously planned day trips in Japan's premier cities, offering a blend of culinary delights, engaging activities, must-see viewpoints, and insider tips to enhance your experience. Each itinerary is crafted to showcase the essence of this main cities, incorporating both renowned attractions and hidden gems. You'll find recommendations for dining—from budget-friendly meals to more lavish options—alongside advice on saving money, information on parking, and the costs associated with each experience. Whether you're drawn to pure nature, historical landmarks, cutting-edge technology, or modern attractions, these day trips are structured to provide a comprehensive and unforgettable exploration of Japan's rich cultural landscape and modern dynamism.

Tokyo Day Trip Itinerary

Morning: Asakusa Exploration

- **Start at Senso-ji Temple:** Tokyo's oldest temple offers a rich cultural and historical experience. Free entrance.
- **Breakfast:** Enjoy a traditional Japanese breakfast at a nearby café. Options range from ¥500 for a simple set to ¥1,500 for a more comprehensive meal including fish, rice, miso soup, and pickles.

Midday: Akihabara Adventure

- **Electronics and Anime:** Dive into the world of electronics, manga, and anime. Exploring the shops is free, but purchases will vary.
- **Lunch:** Try a themed café or a local ramen shop. Meals average ¥800 to ¥1,200.

Afternoon: Shibuya and Harajuku

- **Shibuya Crossing and Hachiko Statue:** Witness the famous scramble crossing. No cost.
- **Takeshita Street in Harajuku:** Explore trendy shops and snack on crepes or other street food, typically under ¥500.
- **Meiji Shrine:** A tranquil escape from the city's bustle. Entrance is free.

Evening: Tokyo Skytree

- **Viewpoint:** End your day with breathtaking views from the Tokyo Skytree. Entry to the first observation deck costs ¥2,060; an additional ¥1,030 for the second deck.
- **Dinner:** Dine in Skytree Town, with options ranging from ¥1,000 for a casual meal to over ¥5,000 for a restaurant with a view.

Saving Money Tips:

- Use a one-day metro pass (around ¥600 to ¥800) for unlimited travel.
- Many attractions offer free admission, focusing your spending on meals and specific experiences.
- Explore on foot where possible to soak in the city's atmosphere without any cost.

Parking Info:

- Parking in Tokyo can be expensive and challenging to find. It's recommended to use public transportation for convenience and savings.

This itinerary combines the traditional charm of Asakusa, the modern otaku culture of Akihabara, the bustling life of Shibuya, and the spectacular views from Tokyo Skytree, ensuring a well-rounded Tokyo experience. From historic sites to modern marvels, this day trip through Tokyo promises a memorable adventure through the city's most iconic landmarks and districts.

Kyoto Day Trip Itinerary

Morning: Fushimi Inari Shrine Visit

- **Activity:** Start your day with a visit to Fushimi Inari Shrine, famous for its thousands of vermilion torii gates.
- **Breakfast:** Grab a traditional Japanese breakfast at a nearby café near Kyoto Station before heading out. Expect to spend around ¥600-¥800 for a set meal featuring rice, miso soup, and grilled fish.

Midday: Explore Arashiyama

- **Activity:** Visit the Arashiyama Bamboo Grove, then walk over to the Tenryu-ji Temple and enjoy the Zen garden.
- **Lunch:** Enjoy soba noodles at a local restaurant in Arashiyama, with meals typically ranging from ¥1,000 to ¥1,500.

Afternoon: Discover Kinkaku-ji and Nijo Castle

- **Activity:** Head to the Golden Pavilion (Kinkaku-ji), then visit Nijo Castle to explore its historic buildings and beautiful gardens.
- **Snack:** Try matcha ice cream or other traditional sweets at shops around Kinkaku-ji, costing about ¥300-¥500.

Evening: Gion District and Dinner

- **Activity:** Stroll through the Gion district, Kyoto's most famous geisha district, and enjoy the traditional architecture.
- **Dinner:** Dine at a restaurant in Gion or Pontocho Alley, where you can find meals ranging from affordable izakaya dishes at around ¥1,500 per person to exquisite kaiseki dinners starting at ¥5,000 and up.

Saving Money Tips:

- Kyoto is best explored on foot or by bus. Consider a one-day bus pass for ¥600 to save on transportation.
- Many temples and shrines have free admission areas, with specific buildings or gardens charging entrance fees.

Parking Info:

- Parking in Kyoto, especially near popular tourist spots, can be scarce and expensive. Public transportation is highly recommended.

This Kyoto day trip itinerary blends the spiritual with the scenic, from the iconic torii gates of Fushimi Inari Shrine to the serene beauty of Arashiyama's bamboo grove, and the historical elegance of Nijo Castle. Culinary experiences range from quick traditional bites to elaborate dinners, offering a taste of Kyoto's rich culinary heritage. With each step, this journey through Kyoto not only unveils the city's most cherished sights but also its hidden corners, making for an unforgettable exploration of Japan's ancient capital.

Osaka Day Trip Itinerary

Morning: Osaka Castle and Surroundings

- **Activity:** Begin your day at Osaka Castle, one of Japan's most famous landmarks, to learn about its history and enjoy the view from the top.
- **Breakfast:** Enjoy a quick and easy breakfast at a café near the castle. Expect to spend around ¥500-¥700 for coffee and a pastry.

Midday: Dotonbori and Shinsaibashi Exploration

- **Activity:** Head to the vibrant Dotonbori area to see the iconic Glico Man sign and explore the bustling Shinsaibashi Shopping Arcade.
- **Lunch:** Try Osaka's famous street food in Dotonbori, such as takoyaki and okonomiyaki, ranging from ¥300 to ¥800.

Afternoon: Umeda Sky Building and Surroundings

- **Activity:** Visit the Umeda Sky Building for panoramic city views from the Floating Garden Observatory. Then, explore the Kita area, known for its shopping and entertainment.
- **Snack:** Grab a coffee or a sweet treat in one of the area's many cafes. Prices for a coffee and a dessert can range from ¥400 to ¥1,000.

Evening: Sumiyoshi Taisha Shrine and Dinner

- **Activity:** As the day winds down, visit Sumiyoshi Taisha Shrine, one of Japan's oldest Shinto shrines, for a peaceful evening stroll.
- **Dinner:** End your day with dinner at a local izakaya in the Tennoji area, where you can enjoy various dishes. Expect to spend ¥1,500 to ¥3,000 per person for a fulfilling meal.

Saving Money Tips:

- Utilize the Osaka Amazing Pass for unlimited subway and bus travel, plus free entry to many attractions.
- Street food in Osaka is not only delicious but also an affordable way to try different local specialties.

Parking Info:

- Parking in central Osaka can be expensive and hard to find. Public transportation is convenient and recommended for day trippers.

This itinerary offers a comprehensive exploration of Osaka, blending historical sites like Osaka Castle and Sumiyoshi Taisha Shrine with the modern vibrancy of Dotonbori and the Umeda Sky Building. From sampling iconic street food to enjoying the city's bustling shopping districts and serene shrines, this day trip through Osaka captures the essence of the city's rich culture, history, and culinary excellence.

Hokkaido, Sapporo Day Trip Itinerary

Morning: Odori Park and Sapporo TV Tower

- **Activity:** Start your day at Odori Park, the green heart of Sapporo, stretching 12 blocks through the city center. Climb the Sapporo TV Tower for panoramic views of the park and the city.
- **Breakfast:** Grab a coffee and a pastry at a nearby café. Expect to spend around ¥500-¥700.

Midday: Historical Village of Hokkaido

- **Activity:** Explore the Historical Village of Hokkaido, an open-air museum showcasing the island's pioneering history. See reconstructed buildings and learn about life in Hokkaido from the Meiji and Taisho eras.
- **Lunch:** Enjoy a meal at a restaurant within the museum or pack a picnic. Restaurant meals average ¥1,000-¥1,500.

Afternoon: Moerenuma Park

- **Activity:** Visit Moerenuma Park, designed by Isamu Noguchi, for its striking modern art installations and beautifully landscaped areas.
- **Snack:** Try soft-serve ice cream made with Hokkaido milk, a local favorite, costing about ¥300-¥400.

Evening: Susukino District

- **Activity:** Explore Susukino, Sapporo's entertainment district, known for its nightlife, restaurants, and neon lights.
- **Dinner:** Dine at a seafood izakaya or a ramen shop, where you can enjoy Sapporo's famous miso ramen. Meals range from ¥800 to ¥2,000 per person.

Saving Money Tips:

- Sapporo's subway system offers one-day passes for unlimited travel, helping to save on transportation costs.
- Many of Sapporo's parks and public spaces are free to enter, offering budget-friendly sightseeing options.

Parking Info:

- Parking in Sapporo can be expensive, especially in the city center. Public transportation is highly recommended for exploring the city efficiently.

This Sapporo day trip itinerary combines the natural beauty of Hokkaido with the city's rich history and vibrant modern culture. From the tranquil greenery of Odori Park and the innovative design of Moerenuma Park to the historical insights at the Historical Village of Hokkaido and the lively atmosphere of Susukino, Sapporo offers a diverse array of experiences that showcase the best of Japan's northernmost prefecture.

Fukuoka Day Trip Itinerary

Morning: Ohori Park and Fukuoka Castle Ruins

- **Activity:** Begin your day at Ohori Park, a peaceful oasis in the city with a large pond and walking paths. Adjacent are the ruins of Fukuoka Castle, offering a glimpse into the city's samurai past.
- **Breakfast:** Enjoy a light breakfast at a café near the park. Expect to spend ¥500-¥700 for coffee and a Japanese-style pastry.

Midday: Hakata Ward and Kushida Shrine

- **Activity:** Explore Hakata, Fukuoka's historic district. Visit Kushida Shrine, a Shinto shrine known for its role in the Hakata Gion Yamakasa festival.
- **Lunch:** Try Hakata ramen, Fukuoka's famous tonkotsu (pork bone broth) ramen, at a local ramen shop. A bowl typically costs around ¥800-¥1,000.

Afternoon: Canal City Hakata

- **Activity:** Head to Canal City Hakata, a large shopping and entertainment complex known for its distinctive architecture and the canal running through it. Catch a free water show and explore the shops.
- **Snack:** Sample some matcha-flavored treats or taiyaki at one of the mall's snack stands, usually around ¥300-¥500.

Evening: Nakasu District

- **Activity:** As the sun sets, visit Nakasu, Fukuoka's nightlife hub, situated on an island in the river. Famous for its yatai (street food stalls), it's a perfect place to enjoy Fukuoka's vibrant food culture.
- **Dinner:** Dine at a yatai, trying dishes like yakitori, tempura, and local specialties. Expect to spend ¥2,000-¥3,000 per person for a

variety of dishes and drinks.

Saving Money Tips:

- Walking or using a day pass for public transport can significantly save on travel costs within Fukuoka.
- Eating at yatai or local ramen shops offers a delicious yet budget-friendly dining experience.

Parking Info:

- Parking in Fukuoka can be challenging and costly, especially near major attractions. Utilizing public transportation or parking on the outskirts and taking the subway or bus is advisable.

This itinerary showcases Fukuoka's blend of natural beauty, historical sites, and modern attractions, from serene parks and ancient shrines to bustling shopping centers and lively street food scenes. Whether exploring the city's rich history or indulging in its renowned culinary delights, a day trip to Fukuoka promises an array of experiences that cater to all interests and tastes.

Nara Day Trip Itinerary

Morning: Nara Park and Todai-ji Temple

- **Activity:** Start your day at Nara Park, famous for its free-roaming deer considered sacred in Shinto religion. Then, visit Todai-ji Temple, home to Japan's largest bronze Buddha statue.
- **Breakfast:** Grab a quick bite near the park. Traditional Japanese breakfast options are available for about ¥600-¥800.

Midday: Kasuga Taisha Shrine

- **Activity:** Explore Kasuga Taisha, a beautiful Shinto shrine known for its hundreds of stone lanterns. The path leading to the shrine is both peaceful and picturesque.
- **Lunch:** Enjoy lunch at one of the traditional restaurants in Nara, offering set meals ranging from ¥1,000 to ¥1,500, featuring local specialties.

Afternoon: Naramachi and Kofuku-ji Temple

- **Activity:** Stroll through Naramachi, the old merchant district, for a glimpse into Nara's past with its preserved machiya houses. Visit Kofuku-ji Temple, with its five-story pagoda.
- **Snack:** Try some mochi or other local sweets available at Naramachi. Prices for snacks are typically around ¥300-¥500.

Evening: Isuien Garden

- **Activity:** Conclude your day with a visit to Isuien Garden, a serene Japanese garden that offers a tranquil escape and beautiful scenery, especially during the autumn and spring.
- **Dinner:** Dine in the Nara town center, where you can find various dining options from izakayas to upscale restaurants. Dinner costs can range from ¥1,500 for a casual meal to ¥3,000 or more for a finer dining experience.

Saving Money Tips:

- Nara's main attractions are relatively close together and can be explored on foot, saving on transportation costs.

- Entrance fees for temples and shrines are modest, but visiting park areas and exploring the town itself is free.

Parking Info:

- Limited and paid parking is available near major attractions. Considering Nara's compact and walkable nature, parking once and walking or using public transportation for longer distances is advisable.

This Nara day trip itinerary offers a blend of cultural heritage, spiritual sites, and natural beauty. From the iconic deer of Nara Park to the historical depths of Todai-ji and the quiet charm of Isuien Garden, Nara presents a peaceful yet enriching experience that captures the essence of ancient Japan.

Kanazawa Day Trip Itinerary

Morning: Kenrokuen Garden and Kanazawa Castle

- **Activity:** Begin your day at Kenrokuen, one of Japan's "three best landscape gardens," famed for its beauty in all seasons. Adjacent is Kanazawa Castle, known for its impressive stone walls and gates.
- **Breakfast:** Sample some local Kaga cuisine for breakfast at a nearby café or restaurant, with prices around ¥700-¥1,000 for a set meal including rice, miso soup, and local fish.

Midday: Higashi Chaya District

- **Activity:** Explore the Higashi Chaya District, a well-preserved area with traditional teahouses and artisan shops. Visit a gold leaf workshop to see a unique aspect of Kanazawa's craft heritage.

- **Lunch:** Enjoy sushi or seafood donburi, highlighting Kanazawa's access to fresh seafood. Expect to spend ¥1,500-¥2,500.

Afternoon: Omicho Market and Nagamachi Samurai District

- **Activity:** Stroll through Omicho Market, known as Kanazawa's kitchen, for fresh produce and seafood. Then, visit the Nagamachi Samurai District to see historic samurai residences.
- **Snack:** Try some local snacks from Omicho Market, like grilled seafood or Kanazawa's famous ice cream topped with gold leaf, typically costing ¥300-¥500.

Evening: 21st Century Museum of Contemporary Art

- **Activity:** Conclude your day with a visit to the 21st Century Museum of Contemporary Art to enjoy modern art installations and exhibitions.
- **Dinner:** Dine in one of the restaurants or izakayas near the museum or in the city center. A casual meal can range from ¥1,000 to ¥2,000, while kaiseki dining starts at ¥5,000.

Saving Money Tips:

- Consider purchasing a one-day bus pass for unlimited travel around the city, which is cost-effective and convenient.
- Many of Kanazawa's attractions, like the Higashi Chaya District and Nagamachi Samurai District, are free to explore on foot.

Parking Info:

- Parking in Kanazawa can be found but is often paid. It's advisable to use public transportation or park in one location and explore nearby attractions on foot to save on costs.

This itinerary for a day trip to Kanazawa blends the city's rich cultural heritage with its vibrant modern attractions. From the serene beauty of Kenrokuen Garden and the historic charm of the Higashi Chaya District to the innovative art at the 21st Century Museum, Kanazawa offers a diverse range of experiences. Sampling the local cuisine, from traditional Kaga dishes to fresh seafood at Omicho Market, adds a flavorful dimension to the journey, making Kanazawa a must-visit destination for those seeking to immerse themselves in Japan's regional diversity.

9

Fun Facts and Unique Experiences in Japan

Japan's rich culture and advanced technology create a fascinating tapestry of experiences and facts that are as intriguing as they are unique. From culinary curiosities to social norms that might raise an eyebrow, Japan offers a plethora of interesting activities suitable for families, kids, and couples alike. Here, we explore some of the most fun facts and unique experiences that make Japan a one-of-a-kind destination.

Square Watermelons

Fact: Grown in glass boxes to adopt a cube shape, these watermelons are designed for easier storage. **Experience:** Spot these in select upscale supermarkets, mainly as decorative items due to their high price.

Capsule Hotels

Fact: Offering compact, pod-sized accommodations, capsule hotels are a testament to Japan's efficient use of space. **Experience:** Perfect for solo travelers or couples looking for a unique lodging experience. Prices range from affordable to mid-range, depending on the hotel's amenities.

Cat Cafes

Fact: Japan's love for cats is epitomized by cat cafes, where guests can enjoy coffee while mingling with feline residents. **Experience:** A relaxing activity for families and couples alike. Entry fees typically include one drink and are priced by the hour.

Rabbit Island (Okunoshima)

Fact: A small island in Hiroshima Prefecture inhabited by hundreds of friendly rabbits. **Experience:** Ideal for animal-loving families and couples. Accessible by ferry, with a small fee for entry.

The Kanamara Matsuri (Penis Festival)

Fact: A unique festival celebrating fertility and good fortune, with phallic imagery and goods. **Experience:** Held annually in Kawasaki, it's a humorous and eye-opening cultural event for adults.

A Lonely Death Cleaning Service

Fact: Specialized services in Japan clean up apartments where individuals have passed away unnoticed, reflecting Japan's aging society. **Experience:** More of a societal observation than an activity, highlighting Japan's unique services catering to demographic challenges.

Vending Machines for Everything

Fact: Japan's vending machines sell a bewildering array of products, from drinks to umbrellas. **Experience:** Discovering unusual vending machines becomes a fun exploration game for visitors.

World's Shortest Escalator

Fact: Located in the basement of More's department store in Kawasaki, this escalator has only five steps. **Experience:** A quirky photo op and a testament to Japan's love for convenience.

Sleeping on the Job is Acceptable

Fact: Inemuri, or sleeping while present, is often seen as a sign of hard work in Japan. **Experience:**Observing this phenomenon offers insight into Japan's work culture.

Slurping Noodles is Polite

Fact: Slurping noodles is considered polite in Japan, indicating enjoyment of the meal. **Experience:** Visitors can embrace this practice at ramen or soba shops, adding to the authentic dining experience.

Adult Adoption

Fact: Japan has a practice of adopting adults, often to preserve family businesses. **Experience:** Learning about this custom sheds light on Japan's approach to business and family legacy.

Toilet Slippers

Fact: Many Japanese homes and traditional establishments provide slippers to be worn exclusively in the toilet. **Experience:** Adhering to this practice is a simple way for visitors to show respect for Japanese customs.

These fun facts and unique experiences showcase Japan's blend of tradition, innovation, and quirkiness, offering endless discovery opportunities for every kind of traveler. Whether you're marveling at agricultural innovations, enjoying the country's animal-themed islands and cafes, or immersing yourself in its distinctive social customs, Japan promises a journey filled with wonder and amusement.

10

100 Tips for an Unforgettable Adventure

Embarking on a journey through a place as Japan offers an array of experiences across the spectrums of nature, technology, culture, and culinary delights. Whether you're a solo traveler, a family with children, a couple, or seeking adventures that fit both modest and luxury budgets, these 100 tips will ensure your Japanese adventure is truly unforgettable.

1. **Learn Basic Phrases:** Knowing simple greetings and phrases in Japanese enhances interactions and shows respect.
2. **Cash is King:** While digital payments are on the rise, cash is still widely used, especially in rural areas.
3. **Rail Pass:** Consider a JR Rail Pass for extensive travel. It can save you money on long-distance trains.
4. **Pack Light:** With lots of walking and stairs, especially in subway stations, light luggage is a must.
5. **Stay Connected:** Rent a pocket Wi-Fi or buy a local SIM card for easy navigation and translation.

6. **Public Transport:** Master the art of using Japan's efficient public transport system, including buses and trains.

7. **Respect Local Customs:** Be mindful of Japanese etiquette, such as bowing, removing shoes indoors, and not tipping.

8. **Convenience Stores:** Utilize convenience stores for cheap, delicious snacks, meals, and ATMs.

9. **Seasonal Highlights:** Plan your visit around seasonal events like cherry blossom viewing in spring or autumn leaves.

10. **Stay in a Ryokan:** Experience traditional Japanese hospitality by staying in a ryokan (inn) at least once.

11. **Onsen Etiquette:** Learn the proper etiquette before enjoying Japan's famous hot springs.

12. **Travel Insurance:** Always have travel insurance for unexpected incidents or medical emergencies.

13. **Layer Clothing:** Weather can change rapidly; layers are essential to adjust to varying temperatures.

14. **Vending Machines:** Use them for quick drinks, snacks, and even umbrellas.

15. **Local Festivals:** Participate in local festivals (matsuri) for unique cultural experiences.

16. **Footwear:** Wear comfortable shoes; you'll be walking a lot.

17. **Photography:** Always ask permission before taking photos of people or private property.

18. **Sushi Etiquette:** Learn the basics, like how to properly use soy sauce and pickled ginger.

19. **Eco-Friendly Practices:** Carry a reusable water bottle and shopping bag to align with Japan's eco-conscious efforts.

20. **Safety:** Japan is one of the safest countries, but always keep an eye on personal belongings.

21. **Avoid Peak Travel Times:** Traveling during off-peak times can save money and reduce crowds.

22. **Language Apps:** Use translation apps to help with language barriers.

23. **Cultural Sensitivity:** Be aware of cultural norms, such as quietness on public transport.

24. **Theme Cafes and Restaurants:** Experience unique dining at animal cafes, robot restaurants, and themed eateries.

25. **Explore Beyond Cities:** Venture into rural Japan for stunning landscapes and traditional experiences.

26. **Karaoke:** Embrace the fun of karaoke in one of the many booths available across cities.

27. **Meal Tickets:** In some restaurants, you'll order and pay via a vending machine at the entrance.

28. **Early Planning:** Book accommodations and experiences well in advance, especially during peak seasons.

29. **Respect Sacred Sites:** Be mindful and respectful when visiting temples, shrines, and sacred areas.

30. **Local Cuisine:** Try regional specialties; each area of Japan has its unique dishes.

31. **Market Visits:** Explore local markets for fresh foods, crafts, and a glimpse into daily life.

32. **Tatami Etiquette:** When in a tatami room, avoid stepping on the edges of the mats and remove shoes.

33. **Imperial Palace Tours:** In Tokyo and Kyoto, reserve a spot for a guided tour of the Imperial Palaces.

34. **Disaster Preparedness:** Familiarize yourself with emergency procedures, especially in earthquake-prone areas.

35. **Souvenir Shopping:** Look for unique local crafts, snacks, and items that aren't available elsewhere.

36. **Museum Passes:** Some cities offer museum passes for discounts on multiple attractions.

37. **Nightlife:** Explore Japan's nightlife, from izakayas to nightclubs,

but always be mindful of the last train times.

38. **Anime and Manga:** Visit Akihabara in Tokyo or the International Manga Museum in Kyoto for anime and manga culture.

39. **Japanese Gardens:** Take time to visit and appreciate the tranquility of Japanese gardens.

40. **Sumo Wrestling:** Try to catch a sumo tournament or visit a sumo stable for a practice session.

41. **Drink Responsibly:** Enjoy Japan's sake, whisky, and other beverages, but drink responsibly.

42. **Cycling:** Rent a bike to explore cities and countryside; it's a popular and eco-friendly way to see Japan.

43. **Beach Destinations:** Visit Okinawa or the Izu Peninsula for beautiful beaches and marine activities.

44. **Historical Trails:** Walk parts of the Nakasendo or Kumano Kodo trails for historical and natural beauty.

45. **Mount Fuji:** Plan a trip to see or climb Mount Fuji, but be aware of the climbing season and weather conditions.

46. **Tea Ceremony:** Experience a traditional tea ceremony to learn about this important aspect of Japanese culture.

47. **Shopping Etiquette:** When receiving or giving items, use both hands as a sign of respect.

48. **Capsule Hotels:** For a unique lodging experience, stay in a capsule hotel for a night.

49. **Seasonal Foods:** Enjoy seasonal foods and fruits; Japan's culinary world is deeply connected to the seasons.

50. **Washlets:** Don't be surprised by the high-tech toilets; take a moment to familiarize yourself with the controls.

51. **Packing:** Remember to bring adapters for Japan's electrical outlets and possibly a portable charger.

52. **Respect for Nature:** Appreciate and respect Japan's deep cultural connection to nature, evident in its parks, gardens, and natural

sites.

53. **Quietness:** Maintain a general level of quietness, especially in public spaces like trains, to respect those around you.

54. **Lost Items:** If you lose something, visit the nearest police box (koban); Japan's lost and found system is highly effective.

55. **Travel Off-Season:** Consider traveling during shoulder seasons (spring and autumn) for fewer crowds and pleasant weather.

56. **Local Sim Card:** A local SIM card is invaluable for data and navigation throughout your trip.

57. **Japanese Baths:** Experience a public bath (sento) or hot spring (onsen), remembering the bathing etiquette.

58. **No Tipping:** Tipping is not customary in Japan and can sometimes be seen as rude.

59. **Festivals:** Participate in or observe Japanese festivals (matsuri) for a vibrant cultural experience.

60. **Stay Hydrated:** Stay hydrated, especially during Japan's hot and humid summers.

61. **Cultural Performances:** Watch traditional performances, such as kabuki or noh, for a unique cultural experience.

62. **Japanese Breakfast:** Try a traditional Japanese breakfast at least once, featuring fish, rice, miso soup, and pickles.

63. **Day Trips:** Use Japan's efficient rail system to take day trips from major cities to explore more of the country.

64. **Guided Tours:** Consider joining a guided tour for insights into Japan's history, culture, and landmarks.

65. **Japanese Snacks:** Try various Japanese snacks and sweets, from Pocky to mochi, available at convenience stores and supermarkets.

66. **Nature Walks:** Japan's national parks and nature reserves offer peaceful walks and stunning scenery.

67. **Travel Apps:** Utilize travel apps for train schedules, navigation, and language translation.

68. **Shrine Visits:** When visiting shrines, follow the cleansing ritual at the entrance for a respectful visit.

69. **Interactive Experiences:** Engage in interactive experiences, from samurai lessons to sushi-making classes.

70. **Accommodation Types:** Explore different types of accommodations, from modern hotels to traditional inns (ryokan).

71. **Japanese Etiquette:** Familiarize yourself with basic Japanese etiquette to navigate social situations smoothly.

72. **Local Beverages:** Sample local beverages, from green tea to sake, each region has its specialties.

73. **Street Food:** Don't miss out on street food, especially at markets and festivals, for delicious and affordable eats.

74. **Luggage Delivery:** Use a luggage delivery service (takkyubin) for convenient travel between destinations.

75. **Cultural Workshops:** Participate in cultural workshops to learn traditional crafts or cooking techniques.

76. **Outdoor Activities:** Japan offers a range of outdoor activities, from skiing in Hokkaido to diving in Okinawa.

77. **Shopping Arcades:** Explore covered shopping arcades (shotengai) for a variety of goods and local atmosphere.

78. **Eco-Friendly Practices:** Adopt eco-friendly practices during your visit, respecting Japan's efforts in sustainability.

79. **Local Interaction:** Engage with locals whenever possible; even simple interactions can enrich your travel experience.

80. **Travel Journals:** Keep a travel journal to record your experiences, sights, and personal reflections.

81. **Japanese Confectionery:** Explore the world of Japanese confectionery, known for its artistry and flavors.

82. **Avoid Rush Hour:** When using public transport, try to avoid rush hour to ensure a more comfortable journey.

83. **Photography Rules:** Be mindful of photography rules, especially

in sacred or restricted areas.

84. **Cultural Respect:** Show respect for Japanese culture and traditions, always seeking to learn and understand.

85. **Plan for Weather:** Check weather forecasts and plan accordingly, especially for outdoor activities and travel.

86. **Emergency Numbers:** Keep a list of emergency numbers, including the nearest embassy or consulate.

87. **Japanese Media:** Watch Japanese films or read literature to deepen your understanding of the culture.

88. **Food Allergies:** Communicate any food allergies clearly; consider carrying a translated allergy card.

89. **Local Timekeeping:** Be punctual; timeliness is an important aspect of Japanese culture.

90. **Seasonal Events:** Look out for seasonal events and activities, which can offer unique experiences.

91. **Night Markets:** Visit night markets in cities like Osaka for food, entertainment, and shopping.

92. **Local Guides:** Hiring a local guide can enhance your visit with personalized insights and access to hidden gems.

93. **Traditional Attire:** Try wearing traditional Japanese attire, such as a kimono or yukata, for a special experience.

94. **Public Behavior:** Avoid loud conversations and disturbances in public places, maintaining harmony.

95. **Religious Practices:** Observe and respect religious practices and ceremonies, understanding their significance.

96. **Sustainable Travel:** Practice sustainable travel habits to help preserve Japan's natural and cultural sites.

97. **Foot Bath:** Enjoy a foot bath (ashiyu) for relaxation, available in some parks and onsen towns.

98. **Gift Giving:** Understand the importance of gift-giving in Japanese culture, especially if visiting someone's home.

99. **Disability Access:** Research accessibility options if traveling with a disability; Japan is progressively improving its facilities.
100. **Open Mind:** Keep an open mind and be ready to embrace new experiences, tastes, cultures and so much more!

Following these tips will ensure that your journey through Japan is not only enjoyable but also respectful and enriching. Japan offers a profound depth of experiences that cater to all interests, from its awe-inspiring natural landscapes and rich historical tapestry to its cutting-edge technology and vibrant modern culture.

11

Conclusion

You have dived into the activities that make Japan a unique and unforgettable destination. It provided practical tips for navigating cities, indulging in local cuisine, and embracing Japan's unique culture, aiming to enhance your adventure whether traveling solo, with family, or as a couple.

Throughout, the focus was on creating meaningful connections and memories, from interacting with locals to exploring off-the-beaten-path gems. The true value of your trip lies in these personal moments and discoveries, beyond just the places you visit.

If this guide has been a helpful companion for you, we'd be very appreciative if you could take a few minutes to leave a review on Amazon. Your insights are invaluable, helping to improve and guide future travelers in their exploration of Japan. As you reflect on your journey, remember that each travel experience is a step towards new understanding and adventures.

ありがとうございます for letting us be a part of your journey.

あとでね (until we meet again)!

12

References

Pretraveller, The Essential Guide to 10 Days in Japan for First Time Visitors. Retrieved February 9, 2024, from https://www.pretraveller.com/10-days-in-japan-first-time-itinerary/

Plaza Homes. (2023, October 31). Moving to Japan: 6 Helpful Tips for Getting Settled. Retrieved February 9, 2024, from https://www.realestate-tokyo.com/living-in-tokyo/japan-info/getting-settled/

Will fly for food, (2023, June 24). Japanese Food: 45 Traditional Dishes to Look for in Japan. Retrieved February 9, 2024, from https://www.willflyforfood.net/the-ultimate-japanese-food-guide-what-to-eat-in-japan-and-where-to-try-them/

Tripadvisor. Things to do in Japan. Retrieved February 9, 2024, from https://www.tripadvisor.com/Attractions-g294232-Activities-Japan.html

Tripadvisor, Top Japan Attractions. Retrieved February 9. 2024, from https://www.tripadvisor.com/Attraction_Products-g294232-t11889-zfg11867-Japan.html

Rough Guides. Japan Travel Tips: 13 things to know before you go. Retrieved February 9, 2024, from https://www.roughguides.com/article/japan-travel-tips/

Japan Today, (2023, August 16). Japanese Technology Trends. Retrieved February 9, 2024, from https://japantoday.com/category/special-promotion/5-japanese-technology-trends-for-2023#:~:text=2023%20is%20an%20exciting%20time,Japan%20as%20we%20approach%202024.

The Planet D Team, (2022, August 30). MIND-BLOWING FACTS ABOUT JAPAN. Retrieved February 9, 2024, from https://theplanetd.com/facts-about-japan/